The Writing Circle

A powerful structure that supports writers and
promotes peer interaction — from brainstorming
and sharing drafts to finding their unique voices
and becoming confident writers

Sylvia Gunnery

Pembroke Publishers Limited

For students and teachers in my writing workshops, with
thanks for helping me to recognize and develop
more effective teaching strategies

Pembroke Publishers
538 Hood Road
Markham, Ontario, Canada L3R 3K9
www.pembrokepublishers.com

Distributed in the U.S. by Stenhouse Publishers
480 Congress Street
Portland, ME 04101
www.stenhouse.com

We acknowledge the financial support of the Government of Canada through the
Book Publishing Industry Development Program (BPIDP) for our publishing
activities.

We acknowledge the Government of Ontario through the Ontario Media
Development Corporation's Ontario Book Initiative.

Library and Archives Canada Cataloguing in Publication

Gunnery, Sylvia
    The writing circle / Sylvia Gunnery.

Includes index.
ISBN 978-1-55138-217-3

    1. English language—Composition and exercises—Study and teaching
(Elementary). 2. English language—Composition and exercises—Study and
teaching (Secondary). 3. Group work in education. I. Title.

LB1631.G863 2007   372.62'3044   C2007-904161-2

Editor: Kate Revington
Cover Design: John Zehethofer
Typesetting: JayTee Graphics

Printed and bound in Canada
9 8 7 6 5 4 3 2 1

Contents

1

A Community of Writers

Think of a book you've read recently. Now, think of the author of this book, busy inside the process of writing it. Are you imagining that author sitting alone at a computer or perhaps leaning intently over a desk, pen scrawling words across a page? Whatever other details you've conjured up, it is most likely that you see this writer alone. We do think of writing as a solitary, even lonely activity. Much of the time within the writing process, this perception may be true; however, it is also true that writers sometimes meet with other writers. They confer with each other, they socialize, they talk about the works of other writers, they discuss publishing, and they share their works-in-progress.

A clear indication that writing is not always solitary is the popularity of writing courses, retreats for writers, and groups that gather for the specific purpose of discussing works-in-progress. The Banff Centre Writing Studio, for example, includes these details in its Web site description: "the program offers an extended period of uninterrupted writing time, one-on-one editorial assistance from experienced writers/editors, and an opportunity to engage with a community of working writers. The Writing Studio is an ideal environment for artistic inspiration and growth." Especially in the early development of writers, much is gained by learning together and inspiring one another.

Curriculum goals in writing can be easily met when students gather in small groups—writing circles—to face the challenges and rewards of writing together. Writing circles in the classroom support writers so that they do not lose confidence, feel blocked by the blank page or the blank screen—or quit. They also provide teachers with more time for assessment and individual instruction. Teachers who use writing circles have more time to notice individual successes and needs, to observe group progress, to teach whole-group or individual lessons, and to join in the activities of the circles.

In our classrooms, writing circles create an active and productive learning environment where our students have many opportunities

- to learn together
- to reinforce what they already know about writing
- to inspire one another to push forward during those solitary times in the writing process

Writing Circles Within the Writing Process

A difficulty in explaining the writing process is that we often make it seem linear and clean: pre-writing, draft writing, researching, conferring, revising, final draft writing, and then publication or sharing. It seems that one thing follows the other until the writer has accomplished a polished and presentable piece. This isn't the case, though—writing creates a mess! And it's the mess that's needed in order for writing to evolve into something "polished and presentable."

All stages of the writing process are tangled and webbed together, with writers moving from one to the other, back again, doing two things at once (or three or more), and probably never truly finishing, just recognizing that they have done all that they can. As students work together in their writing circles, they share experiences and encourage one another to move forward, sideways, and back again through the writing process, all the while moving towards a strong final draft.

Sharing experiences that lead to discoveries

Whether they come together by personal choice or by teacher initiative, writers who meet to develop skills in writing form a writing circle. The writers engage in discussion on a wide range of topics, explore the complexities of the writing process, consider connections between what they read and what they write, and share experiences and works-in-progress. Students in a writing circle ask questions, offer ideas, listen and think, sometimes read aloud, sometimes write together—always furthering their understandings of the writing process and their own writing development.

Writing circle activities allow diverse learners to begin at personal, significant points in their learning and to move forward from there. The writing circle is neither an "enriched" nor a "remedial" experience—it is, at the same time, both these things. The teacher guides students step by step through writing circle lessons to the point where they recognize certain truths about the writing process, about their own writing, and about themselves as writers. Rather than simply be told what works and what doesn't work in writing, students in writing circles share experiences that lead them to discover the fundamentals of writing.

How Writing Circles Address Curriculum Goals

The lessons in this book can easily be adapted for use in Grades 4 to 12.

Numerous curriculum goals related to specific student needs can be achieved in writing circles. Several goals that are developed throughout the lessons in this book are outlined below:

- *generating writing ideas:* An individual may sometimes get bogged down about writing topics even before the writing begins. Informal conversations and guided group activities about personal writing choices help young writers get a feel for what topics are meaningful to them.
- *building self-confidence in writing:* For students, lack of self-confidence often gets in the way of keeping the writing going. At some point in the creative process, everyone has nagging self-doubts. By talking in supportive peer groups and by listening to others who share the same feelings, young writers can get past the doubts.
- *reflecting on writing purposes:* Students become more fully engaged in their writing when they understand their own writing purposes. Writing circle conversations about why someone has written *this* poem, *this*

story, *this* essay, or whatever broadens a student's understandings of personal writing goals.

- *reflecting on writing styles:* Individuals enjoy reading texts by particular authors and enjoy writing on personal themes and in certain genres. In writing circles, all these diverse experiences are shared and considered, so that students think critically about a wider variety of writing styles.
- *making reading–writing connections:* So often, young writers do not easily see ways in which their writing can be strengthened by their reading. Shared activities in writing circles that focus on reading–writing connections provide two valuable opportunities: for students to deepen understanding of how their own reading builds skills in their writing and to enhance their understanding even further by reflecting on the knowledge of others.
- *developing listening and speaking skills:* The essence of writing circles is communication. Students learn to speak clearly, giving effective explanations; they also learn to listen carefully and consider thoughtfully. (See Chapter 2 for more on this.)
- *developing revision skills:* When students work together to help one another see ways in which to develop draft writing, they are more likely to see how to improve their work and to willingly put in the effort to do so. Many young writers view revision as "fixing mistakes" rather than making improvements, so teachers are always looking for ways to encourage them to revisit their writing. It can be less discouraging when others in the writing circle are also going back over their writing to make improvements and corrections.
- *exploring voice:* Within a writing circle are many voices: those personal writer voices developed by each student and those that are chosen to meet specific purposes, such as writing a letter to the editor or a note to a friend. All writers have voice, although it may be caught in clichés rather than strong or unique. Listening to the voices of others—and having others recognize their voices—clarifies and expands students' understanding of author voice.
- *exploring genre:* Individual students have specific preferences in what they enjoy writing. For example, some enjoy writing poetry and may not have considered fantasy fiction. Their experiences widen within the writing circle as they reflect on the works-in-progress of others and as they listen to excerpts of published works used as models.
- *developing skills in usage, grammar, punctuation, and spelling:* Writers learn about conventions and correctness best in the contexts of their own writing and reading. Reading and discussing draft work in writing circles clarify and further expand these skills.
- *sharing works-in-progress:* Students' interest in their works-in-progress can be sparked and renewed through sharing within their small groups. Unfinished manuscripts lie almost forgotten in the bottom drawers of many authors as reminders that when momentum for writing projects is lost, it may never be found. The responses of others can be just the thing to keep writing energy going.

As teachers, we plan our lessons with specific learning goals in mind—and we know that more learning takes place beyond those learning goals. As you work with your students, point out other elements of the writing process that

Voice in writing is the personal "sound" of the writer, usually distinct from the voices of other writers. It is communicated through the tone set by such stylistic elements as word choice, sentence structures, punctuation, imagery, and anecdote. Voice is associated with the topic chosen, the intended audience, and the writer's point of view.

are being reinforced or introduced. If, for example, your students are learning to use anecdotes to support ideas in an essay, you could take an opportunity for them to consider tone—Is the anecdote appropriate to the audience?; organization—Where should the anecdote be placed in the essay?; and word choice—Which words in the anecdote work and which don't? In other words, keep reminding students about the mandatory mess of the writing process.

How to Form Writing Circles

Within a classroom, there may be several writing circles. The number, determined by the teacher, is based on class size and specific student needs. Some students work best in groups of three or four while others are productive in groups of five or six. Although there are both small-group and large-group circles, writing circles work more often with four or five members each. This size provides the potential for more diversity of thought while keeping ideas moving forward—some students are shyer in larger groups. Grouping for learning is widely recognized as a classroom strategy that engages more students.

Small-group circles

As you begin to use writing circles in your classroom, be sure to create varied groupings. Students of diverse interests and abilities can work successfully together in writing circles, respecting their differences and learning from one another. Since the writing process is not a straight line leading to a common end point, individuals in a writing circle have lots of room to offer explanations, ask questions, share drafts, and explore new ideas, no matter what their interests and skills in writing are.

My first realization of this need for diversity was at the Banff Writing Session I attended in the summer of 1976. There were 25 students, ranging in age from 17 to 53. There were poets, fiction writers, and travel writers. There were published authors, writers with suitcases filled with unpublished manuscripts, and those who weren't even sure they wanted to be writers. From my experience, it was the diversity that made this writing group work so well together.

Here are some ideas to consider as you and your students form writing circles in your classroom:

- *class size and classroom size:* Some numbers are easily divided evenly, giving you writing circles with equal numbers. That's not necessary, however. You may have some groups slightly larger than others. Take into consideration the size of your classroom space. Students in writing circles need to hear one another easily. If, for example, you have groups of six meeting in a small space, conditions may not be conducive to discussion. In smaller groups, the talk can be quieter.
- *the time factor:* For ongoing writing projects, your students may be most comfortable staying with the same small grouping throughout. They will get to know each other's works and will grow to trust in one another. On the other hand, you may want students to finish one specific task during a class period. Decide whether the task would be best done within a smaller circle (giving everyone plenty of time to take part) or a larger one (offering as much variety as possible).

- *the lesson topic:* A lesson that asks students to share works-in-progress may work best with groups of three or four so that everyone has enough time to share and to listen to the responses of others in a class period of 30 to 40 minutes. On the other hand, larger writing circles offer more opportunities for learning when there is a lesson focus, for example, on vocabulary development.
- *individual student support:* Some students will need your support as they work in their writing circles. By placing these students randomly throughout the circles, you will more easily be able to observe those students and to offer support when needed.
- *personalities:* You will know who will work cooperatively and who won't. If certain personalities conflict, help them to avoid problems by placing them in different writing circles. There may be opportunities to encourage these conflicting individuals to sort out the difficulties so that they can work together eventually. There's just no point starting out with a known problem.
- *comfort level:* Keep in mind that the nature of writing may have an impact on how writing circles are created. Because writing is such a personal thing—an expression of one's innermost thoughts and imaginings—students may feel most comfortable forming writing circles with particular classmates. This usually works just fine.

Once students have gained a clear sense of direction inside the writing process and can see lots of ways to benefit from taking part in writing circles, there should be less need for teachers to guide the circles.

Sometimes, it works well for good friends to be part of the same writing circle; at other times, it doesn't. A concern is that students may need to find a balance between fun and classroom productivity. If that becomes an issue, make changes in that group, offering students an opportunity to form a writing circle together the next day or the next week. Eventually, students will get the idea.

You may want to change the group members after each activity. One way to create groups is to have students number off, perhaps from 1 to 6. All the number 1s would form a writing circle, the number 2s another, and so on. You can discreetly influence the make-up of groups by having students number off as you point to each person.

Eventually, both you and your students will be comfortable enough for them to form their own writing circles, especially when they have their own purposes. For example, one writing circle may gather for half an hour to discuss someone's work-in-progress while other students, having no reasons to meet at that time, write independently. It may take four to six weeks to establish the purposes and functions of writing circles in a classroom so that students are clear about them. The enthusiasm and professionalism of the teacher are key to bringing students to this point of independence.

All writers benefit from hearing the works and views of people they may not otherwise choose to be in their group. Often the very fact of the group's diversity enhances the learning: a personal view is expanded when an idea is expressed from another point of view; a deeper understanding of the writing process can be achieved when observing various examples and approaches. A student, for instance, may be highly skilled in descriptive writing, yet fall into the pattern of choosing words overzealously from a thesaurus. When sharing aloud descriptions that are clumsy with distracting adjectives and adverbs, this student would readily learn from peers in a writing circle discussion.

9

Whole-class circle

By thinking of the whole class as a circle, teachers are reminded that the students are the focus of the lesson and that they themselves are part of the circle, introducing a topic, guiding the lesson, still encouraging students to explore and share.

There will be times when you will want all your students involved in the same writing circle. You may find this especially effective when you are introducing a new topic, perhaps voice in writing. Or, you may want to involve everyone in a mini-lesson about a correctness matter, for example. It may take only five minutes to consider such techniques as using exclamation marks, bold print, or capital letters to show emphasis.

A whole-class circle can also be a good strategy to use near the end of a writing class: it gives students a chance to share what they have learned in their smaller writing circles or to ask questions that arose in the group work. For example, after a lesson on the advantages of reading draft writing aloud, one student asked the class, "Why can't I notice mistakes as soon as I write them down?" Another student commented, "If I don't read my story out loud, it's like my mind can't hear that I wrote the same thing a couple of times."

Although it is unnecessary that students form a physical circle for these whole-class discussions, it is important that everyone can easily see and hear each speaker. Plan to give a few moments for all students to refocus from their small-group work to the larger group. The best way to begin the transition from smaller writing circles to the larger one is to briefly visit each group to ask if they have achieved their task and to let them know the focus is soon going to change.

Quiet isn't always instant. Try not to add to the noise by raising your own voice for attention; simply revisit the groups that are still engaged and ask if they're ready to share. Once the sharing has begun, students may choose to stand; however, be sure to make standing a choice rather than a requirement because shy students may avoid offering ideas if they must be in the limelight.

A Significant Shift in Focus

Your students may want to expand their writing circles by setting up a blog with your guidance. Within this Internet writing community, bloggers would post writing and invite comments.

Writing circles give individual students more opportunities to find the best time to learn. Traditionally, teachers decided that everyone would learn the same thing in the same way on the same day. We've moved away from that, now offering various strategies that encourage diversity in our classrooms.

As educators, we know the curriculum goals that must be met, we have vast personal experience in all the various aspects of language arts, and we recognize the diversity of student talents and needs in our classrooms. But we can't know precisely the best time for every student to reflect on, to explore, and to learn about specific concepts.

Writing circles help us address the diversity in our classrooms. When students work in writing circles, the teacher's roles are much the same as in any other writing class: to organize, plan, listen, observe, explain, question, encourage, write, read, and lots more. The *difference* is that writing circles pull the focus away from the teacher to a small-group focus on students. This difference is significant.

Although the focus shifts, teachers still have important work to do:

- *to organize and plan:* The students need to know why they are meeting, and most often this is determined by you, the teacher. Eventually, though, students will want to set specific goals for their writing circles.
- *to listen and observe:* Notice who is speaking and who is not, and notice what individuals are saying. Sometimes, sit within a writing circle and take part; other times, move quietly about the room, listening and observing. Briefly note what you observe for evaluation and assessment purposes. One style of note sheet, which incorporates a system of plus and minus signs for quick reference, is shown below.

<table>
<tr><td colspan="3">*Writing Circles*
Date: _____</td></tr>
<tr><td>**Student Name**</td><td>**Writing Activity**</td><td>Notations</td></tr>
<tr><td>**Lily**</td><td>**recognizing voice**</td><td>**+ explained how she wants her story to be told in voice of teenaged boy**</td></tr>
<tr><td>**Dan**</td><td>**(same)**</td><td>**++ explained one author's voice using first page of a novel**</td></tr>
<tr><td>**Wendy**</td><td>**sharing her story**</td><td>**– needs help with how to indicate a flashback**</td></tr>
</table>

As the reference to *same* suggests, all writing circles may not be focused on the same activity in any one class. The first two students on which the teacher made notations belong to the same circle focused on voice; the third was reading her story aloud to her writing circle and asking for comments on the scene changes.

- *to explain, question, and encourage:* It may be appropriate to interrupt a discussion and make a suggestion, perhaps offering a writing resource book for reference or providing an explanation that will move the conversation forward more smoothly. An overheard comment may inspire a teacher-generated question that the writing circle would benefit from discussing. A simple "Interesting" or "I never thought of that" can encourage students to stay focused on the writing circle. At times, when small-group writing circles have completed the day's activities, you may want to invite one or two students to share with the whole class specific observations, questions, or comments overheard. Doing so can be an effective way to further develop a topic or to introduce a new one. Often, young people are more receptive to ideas that are student generated.
- *to write and read:* When you invite your students to write and read, join them as often as you can. During a brief period of quiet reading or writing, you may take part as well. Why do teachers feel a pang of guilt when enjoying reading and writing with our students? There's no need for that guilt. When we show our students that we too enjoy and sometimes struggle with reading and writing, we're doing the best job of modelling for them. Our *primary* responsibility though is to observe, listen, and assess during small-group sessions.

Specific roles for students

As you begin to familiarize your students with writing circles, you may find it useful to define specific roles for them. Just as there are often specific roles in such groups as Literature Circles, there are roles common to writing circles:

- a discussion leader, who keeps everyone on topic and makes sure that everyone has a chance to speak
- a time keeper, who works within the time parameters set by the teacher and lets everyone know how much time is remaining for the activity
- a note taker, who records a few notable ideas
- a speaker, who will report to the whole class a few of the notable ideas
- a reader, who reads aloud any texts of relevance to the writing circle activity, such as encyclopedia or dictionary notations
- a checker, who uses writing resources to check for correctness when the writing circle is creating a display or a written report
- an illustrator, who creates the image(s) for any displays

All members can help with illustration by suggesting content, finding printed images, making headings, writing captions, adding color, and so on.

You may want to distribute role cards such as those on pages 13 and 14. (The front of each card names the role; the back of each card defines the role.) More than one task may be done by each student. The role cards can be distributed randomly, or students may volunteer for specific roles offered by the discussion leaders. Eventually, students will understand how to contribute to a writing circle, and specific tasks may not need to be assigned.

Not all these roles are needed each time the writing circles meet—roles depend on the purpose of the activity. Teacher-designed lessons are more likely to use the roles; however, when students form more informal writing circles to share writing, the roles are usually unnecessary.

Unique Discoveries, Common Goals

Writing circles make any classroom a busy place. Reading aloud, writing, rewriting, talking, reflecting, questioning, and all other activities involved in the writing process may be happening at the same time. Each writing circle has an energy and a purpose of its own—students get to know one another in this new context and quickly recognize that they share common goals.

As you move from circle to circle, or as you observe a group from a distance, you will be able to identify the focus students have taken. Perhaps the activity is teacher directed. Even so, the writing circles won't be in sync. Instead, they will have directions and discoveries unique to each of them. That's part of the fun for the teacher: eavesdropping, adding an idea here and there, asking a question, noting something that would interest the rest of the class, sitting with a group to listen to their understandings develop.

When you are observing all those writing circles, the level of engagement is easily determined. You will find that high levels of engagement are the norm; however, it is not hard to refocus a writing circle that becomes distracted. There is usually at least one person in the group who will lead the way back to the task at hand, especially with a gentle hint from the teacher.

When all the elements of the writing circle are established and students are working together on meaningful writing projects, it's a joy to be a teacher in that busy classroom.

Writing Circle Role Cards

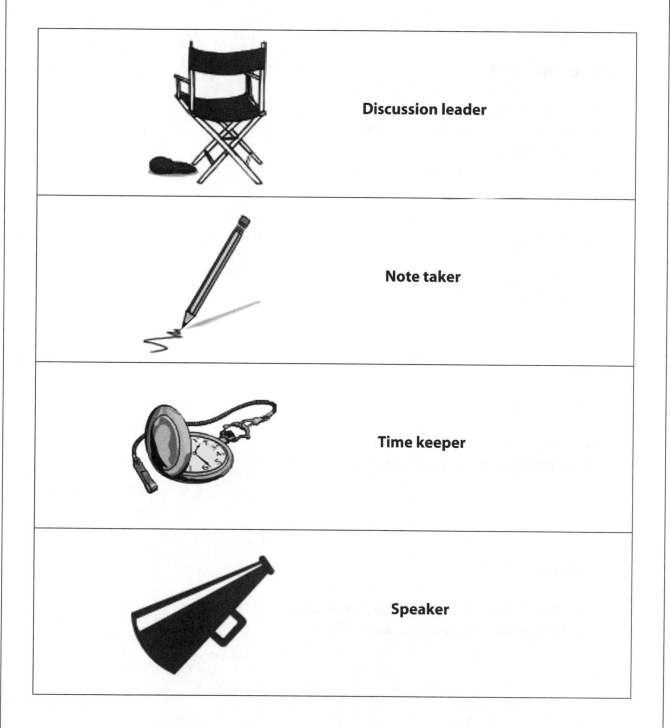

Discussion leader

Note taker

Time keeper

Speaker

Copy pages 13 and 14 back to back to create four cards, one set for each writing circle, if desired.

Discussion leader

Offers jobs to group members
Encourages everyone to speak and to listen
Asks questions
Moves conversation along

Note taker

Records highlights of conversation
for use in sharing with whole class

Time keeper

Keeps track of time for the given task
Occasionally reminds group of time remaining

Speaker

Uses the note taker's highlights of conversation
Explains the points group decides to share

2

2

Within the Writing Circle

As explained in Chapter 1, writing circles involve more than students commenting on the writing of others. For example, together, members of a writing circle may explore a topic that will build on their own writing, perhaps learning about writing resources, considering strong beginnings in published works, and sharing visuals that represent ideas in the writing. This is the case in many of the lessons in this book.

Writing circles focus on pieces of writing as they evolve from glimmer of idea through draft and revision to polished works. Members constructively look at works-in-progress. The emphasis is on process over product.

Given that focus, it is essential that writing circle members offer clear and helpful ideas. Often, friends will instinctively offer platitudes, such as "That's good writing" or "I really like that"; however, such statements are neither clear nor helpful. Writers need to know the truth about what works and what does not; they also need to know specific details so that they fully understand. Otherwise, they will get nowhere in their development as writers.

It is also true that writers—inexperienced and experienced alike—are sometimes very sensitive about correction and criticism of their works. That sensitivity comes from doubt, and that doubt is tied up in ownership. It isn't unique to draft writing, though. Think of new haircuts or particular ways of dressing. When a comment is made to suggest change—"Why don't you try this cut?" or "How about wearing this shirt instead?"—the sensitivity is there, squirming.

So, it's important to "tread softly" by offering honest suggestions in a thoughtful way.

Ideas on Responding to Works-in-Progress

The following are strategies that you'll want your students to know and use when responding to works-in-progress in writing circles. You may want to provide students with an overview of the strategies so that they can refer to them as they build their skills in the area. A handout summarizing the advice appears at the end of the chapter. Related lessons are offered in Chapter 3.

Begin positively

The best way to open any discussion about writing is with a positive comment. This sets the tone of the conversation and can give the writer a boost of confidence in what can often be an awkward situation—sharing one's writing isn't always easy. Here's an example of a clear constructive comment: "The

How to Respond to a Work-in-Progress

Begin positively.
Listen thoughtfully.
Ask the writer to read aloud.
Read aloud from the
    work-in-progress.
Be truthful and tactful.
Make your response constructive.
Limit what you say.
Do not tell a writer what to write.

action on page 2 really got me interested. Maybe that scene could go before the description on page 1 so the reader gets into the story faster."

Students need to realize that even a single effective word choice is worth talking about, for example: "In your description of the puppies, I liked how you wrote 'clumsy bundle' because it gives a great picture of how uncoordinated little dogs are and how they all stay together."

If a student can find nothing positive to say, remaining silent is an option. Others in the writing circle may have noticed something to discuss.

Listen thoughtfully

As writing is read aloud to the group—or as students silently read the works of another—it is important to concentrate. Students should think about how the writing affects them or how it might affect other readers. Their "gut reactions" or first impressions are important.

Ask the writer to read aloud

Instead of jumping in with a comment, a member of a writing circle may ask the writer to choose a scene and read it aloud. The conversation may begin with the writer pointing out what seems to be strong writing. When a writer is asked to choose a scene he or she feels good about, the positive responses can be a boost before any unsuccessful parts are discussed.

Read aloud from the work-in-progress

Alternatively, a writer may say to the other students in the circle: "Listen. This doesn't sound right and I can't figure out why." Circle members would then respond.

It is a powerful experience for writers to hear their writing read aloud by someone else. In a writing circle, a student may volunteer to read aloud a scene that someone finds effective. The reader must rehearse the text enough not to stumble, especially through those places where things have been scratched out or rearranged. Sometimes, that student comes to the teacher or to a friend for some coaching—a great opportunity to build upon reading skills. The reader could then point out specific details that contributed to the strength of the writing.

Be truthful and tactful

When students are asked to respond to writing, it is best to do so with honesty. False praise is never helpful to a writer. If they "begin positively," then the writer is likely to be more open to any criticisms.

However, students should always be considerate and polite. For example, someone may want to point out that the opening scene didn't catch his interest. Rather than bluntly saying that the opening is "boring," the circle member could let the writer know the point at which the writing did catch his interest. If that happens to be in the second paragraph or on the second page, the writer will understand that the opening just didn't work.

Make your response constructive

Authors don't get the chance to go back and make their writing stronger once they have been published; in the classroom, though, students are working through the process, looking for ways in which to improve their work and hoping that conversations with peers and teachers will help them do just that. They still have a chance to incorporate suggestions that work for them.

Students benefit from realizing that it is sometimes helpful to begin a criticism of a work-in-progress in these ways:

- "When you do your next draft, you could think about ..."
- "Before you finish this scene, ask yourself ..."

These kinds of comments leave plenty of room for the writer to consider writing that doesn't work for specific reasons. They are reminders that the writing is not finished: that the ideas, sentence structure, and words are still inside the process.

In contrast, if a response implies that the writer has somehow failed irrevocably, it becomes a roadblock in the writing process. Consider the difference between these two comments:

- "The first scene about getting ready for the fishing trip isn't interesting and doesn't have anything to do with the boating accident."
- "The boating accident is the most exciting scene in your story. When you do your next draft, you could think about whether all the scenes build up to that point. Cut the ones that slow things down too much."

The writer who hears or reads the first response would probably feel defeated and would also not gain any sense of how revision could solve the problem. A response such as the second is much more supportive. It offers a revision strategy, yet does not tell the writer what to write.

Limit what you say

Encourage students to determine the best response to offer the writer. It's not necessary to speak about all the ways in which the writing affects them—they need to choose carefully. A student may begin by talking about one thing she enjoyed and quoting a specific brief passage. For example: "The way you described the lake, I could imagine being there—'the mist hung over the mirror of the lake.'" She could then offer a specific question for the writer to consider in revision: "In the scene where the moon comes up and the campers decide to search for the person who disappeared, did you want that part to seem like they're feeling hopeless or feeling determined?"

Do not tell a writer what to write

Students need to know that they should refrain from suggesting specific words, plot details, and more to their peers. Reacting to what has been written is best without taking the "what if you did this ..." approach in the early development stages for writers. When students have written something that just doesn't work, they seem to get the idea really quickly and move on to something else. Telling writers what to write may seem a lot like telling them what clothes to wear or how to style their hair—it is too personal and is only one opinion. The writer decides what works and what doesn't.

A related issue is that young writers (and probably many adult writers) may not have enough self-confidence to let someone know that a suggestion doesn't work. It's also possible that the original is better!

Ideas on Sharing Works-in-Progress

The following are strategies you'll want your students to know and use when sharing their works-in-progress in writing circles. You may want to provide your students with an overview of the strategies so that they can refer to them

A less experienced student might not be as articulate, but could still make the same constructive point: "I wasn't sure what your story was going to be about at first. Maybe you don't need the part about getting ready for the fishing trip."

How to Share a Work-in-Progress
Decide what you want to know.
Organize your pages.
Practise for reading aloud.
Choose your time.
Choose your audience.
Choose the way you will share your
  writing.

Depending on the genre of writing, each writing circle could brainstorm a list of questions from which to choose when sharing works-in-progress. The list of questions could be kept in everyone's Writer's Journal for quick reference. (See "Keeping a Writer's Journal" on pages 19 and 20.)

as they gain experience and build up their skills in this area. A handout summarizing the advice appears at the end of the chapter. Related lessons are offered in Chapter 3.

Decide what you want to know

Responses from others are so important to the development of all writers. Writers need to know if they have communicated what they set out to do in the way they set out to do it. They need to know how their writing affects others.

When students are preparing to share their works in a writing circle, have them first make a brief list of questions they would like the others to consider. For example, in writing fiction a student might ask these questions:

- What kind of person does my main character seem to be?
- Did that first paragraph make you want to read on?
- Did you notice any hints about what might happen next?
- Did you guess the ending ahead of time?
- Did the ending connect clearly to the ideas in my story? Did it disappoint you?

Organize your pages

Often, works-in-progress will be very messy because of the many revisions done. Students may want to create clean, word-processed copies with all the latest revisions in place. Or, they may carefully organize their pages, numbering any paragraph changes and neatly crossing out any sections they want deleted. This clear organization will help writers and circle members to follow the order of the writing when reading.

Practise for reading aloud

Encourage students to read over their writing, making sure that they will be able to read it aloud as well as they can. They will want their audience to enjoy a smooth, confident reading with just the right pace and expression. Although reading aloud is only an option, most students choose it, especially as they gain experience with the writing circle, listening to others share.

Choose your time

Not everyone is ready to share writing at the same time. Each person must decide when the responses of other students would be helpful. Many writers prefer to keep the writing to themselves until it's in the late draft stages. Ensure that students understand that they can choose a time when they feel confident about their writing or when they are stuck and may benefit from the input of others.

Choose your audience

A writing circle offers the opportunity for students to gain a variety of responses to their works-in-progress. However, if students are uncomfortable with the people who are responding to their writing, they likely won't learn much from the experience. As noted earlier, the comfort level is a key factor in the success of a writing circle, so most of the time, let students form their own circles. A student may invite two or three peers to come together for a 15-minute sharing and discussion; alternatively, you may ask students to stay in the same writing circle throughout a specific project. Monitor how well groups are working and encourage gender mixes.

There may be times when a student really wants only the response of one other person—another student or the teacher. Although this is more limited than the writing circle, it is another valid option.

Choose the way you will share your writing

There are a couple of options from which students may choose when deciding to share works-in-progress. They may create a few questions to ask about a specific piece of writing and then invite a small group of people to form a writing circle. At the same time, other class members may be writing, reading, discussing in writing circles, and meeting with the teacher.

In the writing circle, a student may do one of the following:

- Read aloud to the group and then ask questions. In a Writer's Journal (described more fully below), the student could make notes on any comments to consider further.
- Give everyone a copy of the writing or an excerpt to read silently. The student then asks questions and makes notes on comments to consider further.
- Give everyone a copy of the writing or an excerpt to read silently and a copy of the questions to answer in writing, too. In this instance, the teacher should caution the student to limit questions to one or two and not expect extensive answers—the other writers will need to get back to their own writing before too long.

Keeping a Writer's Journal

Throughout writing circle activities, it is highly useful and valuable for each student to keep a Writer's Journal. Students use these journals both during and between their writing circle meetings. Although the composition of circles and writing tasks change, the journals offer continuity.

A Writer's Journal provides an opportunity for students to reflect on their experiences, ask questions, and clarify their understandings. These notes are valuable

- as a record of ideas discussed
- as a way to further clarify ideas
- as a reminder of tasks to do
- as a storage place for writing topics and research
- as an indication of individual student progress
- as an opportunity for further discussion and teaching

You may, at times, want students to consider specific teacher-generated questions following a writing circle activity. After a lesson on writing resources, for example, you could ask students to decide which resource they personally find most useful and give two reasons why. Or, you may simply request that students make notes about significant ideas or questions that come out of their writing circle experiences.

When you introduce the Writer's Journal, ensure that students are familiar with the concept. Journals can be kept in binders or scribblers. Many students like to use large binders that include both their writing and their journals. It's best to introduce the journals before writing circles are established; then, as the circles are introduced, students would begin to make notes, such as those on writing circle rules (described next chapter).

Invite students to make personalized covers for their journals. They may want to draw illustrations or cut and paste images from magazines or computer files. These illustrations often make a student's Writer's Journal and its purposes more meaningful to the young writer.

Assessing Participation in a Writing Circle

As indicated earlier in this chapter, journals can be used by the teacher to comment on student progress.

Periodically, it is useful for students to assess participation in their writing circles. This need not be a complicated process. They could be asked to write brief notes in their journals to explain one thing they did well in their writing circles and one way in which they could improve. One of my students, for example, saw herself as a leader and needed quite a bit of coaching from me to understand that sometimes others would be in charge of writing circle activities. The student, Karolyn, was very pleased to write a note explaining how she had listened well and commented without taking over from the discussion leader; she even mentioned she had more time for thinking when she wasn't the leader. Another student, Chris, always wanted to tease whenever his buddy expressed an idea, but finally realized the teasing was holding up the progress of the whole group and recorded that in his journal.

You may also want an overview of how students perceive the participation of others in their writing circles. Ask them to write brief notes to you, on separate pieces of paper, complimenting any one person in their writing circles for a specific reason. For example, the student who was always teased, Marty, wrote about how, finally, Chris hadn't teased him during the whole class. Another student, Roxanne, once submitted a note to say that Karolyn, who saw herself as a leader, was the best listener because she could remember whole lines of Roxanne's poem. In another instance, a student, Ben, wrote: "I like the time Janice took to answer my question about how effective my ending was. It was really helpful to know that."

It would be worthwhile to share these compliments; however, awkwardness would be avoided if the names were not revealed. Students would come to understand the kinds of things their classmates appreciate when working in writing circles.

When to ask for these assessments depends on your goal. I recommend doing it once a week at first as a way of reinforcing best behavior; after that, especially if it's obvious that everyone "gets it," consider doing it once a month or waiting even longer. Yet, in a very successful writing workshop, I have sometimes invited students to make these assessments so everyone would get a kind of standing ovation for great communication and interaction within their writing circles.

Responding in Writing Circles

Use these strategies when responding to works-in-progress in your writing circles.

Begin positively.

> Comment on writing successes.
> Help to put the writer at ease.

Listen thoughtfully.

> Concentrate on the reading.
> Consider what works and what doesn't.

Invite the writer to read aloud.

> Ask a writer to choose an effective scene to read aloud.

Read aloud from the work-in-progress.

> Ask a writer for permission to read aloud a strong scene.

Be truthful and tactful.

> Give sincere praise—false praise is not helpful.
> Be considerate and polite.

Make your response constructive.

> Remember that the writing is not finished and that the writer is looking for ways to improve it.
> Be supportive and offer a revision idea without telling the writer what to do: "When you do your next draft, you could think about …"

Limit what you say.

> Explain one thing you enjoyed.
> Consider offering a question that suggests revision.

Do not tell a writer what to write.

> Remember that the writer is in charge of choosing what to say.

Sharing in Writing Circles

Use these strategies when sharing your works-in-progress in writing circles.

Decide what you want to know.

> Make a brief list of questions for others to consider.

Organize your writing.

> Be sure that your draft writing is clear and well organized.

Practise for reading aloud.

> Read over your writing before reading aloud the whole thing or an excerpt.

Choose your time.

> Feel confident about your writing.
> Be ready for the responses of others.

Choose your audience.

> You may form a writing circle of people you trust.
> You may meet with one classmate or with your teacher.

Choose how you will share your writing.

> Read aloud and ask questions.
> Give copies for silent reading and then lead a discussion.
> Give copies for silent reading and then ask for written responses.

3

Establishing Writing Circles

Writing circles will be most worthwhile if your students have an opportunity to think about what they are for and how each person can help make them work.

This chapter offers lessons that you may choose from or adapt to your own purposes as you establish writing circles in your classroom. Each lesson provides students with experiences that develop their understanding of writing circles, builds upon what they know about writing and about themselves as writers, and helps them make clear connections between reading and writing.

Explain to your class how you plan to use writing circles as a way of developing individual writing skills. You may want to describe a specific writers' group where writers learn together in your own community or make a display of brochures or Web site pages that give details about writers' groups or retreats. A quick Web search for "writing circles" will provide you with national and international examples to share with your students.

What "Real" Writers Do

Students will recognize that what you're asking them to do in their writing circles is what "real" writers do as they learn together. In other words, they will quickly understand that being a member of a writing circle is an authentic writing experience. Learners are often more readily engaged and more willing to see an activity as worthwhile when they see clear connections to "real-world" experiences.

Informal discussion offers a way for individuals to become familiar with a new concept or classroom strategy. If each person finds a beginning point, discussion will be more meaningful. By considering phrases from several writing groups, your students will further develop their understandings about how writers learn to be writers. Be sure to look at descriptions of any writing courses or circles in or near your own community for ideas, too.

Learning Goal: To familiarize your students with some of the ways in which writers learn to develop their writing skills: independent writing time, small-group instruction, and interaction with other writers

Part 1: Individual Thoughts

Display ideas such as those that follow and read them aloud to your class.

Most writers had been self-taught, slowly learning their craft alone.
—University of British Columbia Writing Course

… an opportunity to engage with a community of working writers. The Writing Studio is an ideal environment for artistic inspiration and growth.
—Banff Centre Writing Studio

lively conversation and creative response
—Martha's Vineyard Summer Institute

benefit from small group workshops
—The Great Blue Heron Writing Workshop

Then, ask students, individually, to consider all the ideas presented and to select one word or phrase that stands out as especially significant. Prompt them to record their ideas in their journals. A student, for example, may choose "lively conversation and creative response."

Next, ask everyone to write a single sentence to explain the significance of the idea chosen. For example, a student may explain "lively conversation and creative response" in this way: "Talking about writing with other writers can help you get interesting ideas and understand more about writing."

Part 2: Sharing Ideas

Invite students to form groups of four or five and share with one another the ideas they recorded in their journals. This activity will not only give everyone an opportunity to think about writing, but it will also provide an introductory writing circle experience.

Conclude by drawing attention to "community of working writers," given that this idea has specific connections to the writing circles. Ask for comments or questions. Point out that each writing circle formed in your classroom represents a "community of working writers." Although it is a simple idea, it is powerful when we refer to our students as writers—this affirms that they *are* writers. Whether they are published authors or not, students are engaged in the writing process and have meaningful writing purposes and personal goals. The emphasis on *working* writers points to their need to understand that good writing demands hard work.

Setting Writing Circle Rules

One way to ensure that your students think about their roles is to invite them to define a set of classroom rules.

Learning Goal: To establish specific expectations for student behavior in writing circles

Part 1: Brainstorming Rule Ideas

Invite your class to brainstorm together, having one student record all suggestions on a flip chart. Students could generate a brainstorm list that looks something like the one below. Typically, about half the rules are negative, half positive, and they reflect a balance. For example, one student says, "Don't talk too much" and another responds with "Make sure you say something."

> *Possible Writing Circle Rules*
>
> **Listen.**
> **Be serious.**
> **Don't interrupt.**
> **Don't talk too much.**
> **Make sure you say something.**
> **Don't be too serious.**
> **No put downs.**
> **Don't make fun of people.**
> **No cell phones or text messaging.**
> **Stay on topic.**
> **Pay attention.**
> **Keep your sense of humor.**
> **Don't leave the room.**

Narrow the list by asking students to write down their first four choices for rules. Then, count the number of "points" earned for each rule.

Part 2: Creating a Set of Rules

From this tally, decide on four to six rules that everyone agrees to follow. The list may look something like this:

> *Our Writing Circle Rules*
>
> **Listen.**
> **Don't talk too much.**
> **Make sure you say something.**
> **No put downs.**
> **Stay on topic.**
> **Keep your sense of humor.**

Post this new set of writing circle rules on a display in your classroom, or distribute them so that each student has a copy to save in his or her journal. Of course, if you teach more than one class, a different set of rules would be created for each class. Even though the rules would turn out to be very similar, it's important for students to take ownership of them.

Part 3: Using the Rules

Ask students to use this set of rules for self-assessment following some writing circle activities. It is recommended that students do this self-assessment for perhaps two or three classes in a row to emphasize the importance of respecting the rules. Then, you can decide when to repeat the self-assessments —sometimes you will want only one or a few individuals to review their behavior in the writing circles; at other times, it will be important for the whole class to take part. These self-assessments will help to reinforce behavior that contributes positively to the writing circles.

Voicing Views About Writing

Although they won't know the same things in the same ways, your students already know a lot about writing. By voicing personal views about it, they will become engaged writers and will begin to see how many similarities are inside a "community of writers."

The lesson outlined below works well to get students thinking about the writing process. The ideas are offered anonymously so students won't feel self-conscious. There is no awkward silence, either, because students give their views on someone else's ideas. Students also gain an opportunity to hear their own views expressed by others—a powerful chance for self-reflection.

The views are expressed briefly—a word, a phrase, or a sentence. The skilled writer can make thoughtful word choices to express complex ideas succinctly while the less skilled writer will be able to express basic ideas simply.

Learning Goals: To reflect on personal likes and dislikes about writing; to consider how the views of others are the same as or different from personal views

Part 1: Personal Likes and Dislikes

Give each student and yourself two sticky notes of different colors.

Select one of the colors and invite everyone to write on the sticky note a word, a phrase, or a sentence that expresses something she or he doesn't like about writing. No names are to be written on the notes.

Give a few minutes for quiet writing time.

Then, each person takes the note and posts it with the others on a flip chart or a chalkboard. This activity creates a one-color display of things some people don't like about writing.

Using the other color sticky note, everyone writes a word, a phrase, or a sentence that expresses something he or she really enjoys about writing. Again, no names are to be written on the notes and the notes are posted to form a display.

Part 2: Sharing Ideas in a Writing Circle

When the two displays have been created, ask every student to select two sticky notes from the displays—one of each color; however, students cannot select their own notes.

Ask students to form writing circles of four or five persons. They will take turns sharing the ideas on the notes, beginning with what everyone doesn't like about writing. Each student is expected to

- read aloud the exact word(s) written on the note
- provide a personal view of the same idea
- let others in the circle add their comments

Students continue the work in their writing circles by next using the notes about what people really enjoy about writing.

As students in writing circles discuss the ideas on the sticky notes, you will be free to walk around and eavesdrop on the conversations. Occasionally, sit within a circle and take part in the process with your students.

When all the notes have been presented and discussed, ask students to put them back in the display area. This display is worth keeping for a while. You may find that, over the next few days, people will visit the display and take a look at some of the notes they had not had a chance to talk about in their own writing circles.

Writing circle members can take turns randomly, or you can suggest that they take turns alphabetically, using their first names (or the names of their favorite authors, for example). Even if there's chatting or laughter as they work this out, it's part of the warm-up to the conversation.

Part 3: Journal Entries

Ask your students to write in their journals one significant point from their discussions. For example:

I'm not the only one who hates fixing mistakes. Practically everyone does. Writing ideas in the first draft is the exciting part. It takes so long to look up words or put in all the commas and stuff. But how else can you get published?

Journal notes may also provide an opportunity for you to have a discussion with individual writers or to clarify any misunderstandings. For example:

I like writing stories once I get going. But it's hard to get good ideas to write about. Everything I write is like some TV show everyone saw. Boring.

That student would likely benefit from some discussion about how to avoid plagiarism or trust in one's own ideas.

Part 4: Self-Assessment

Near the end of this lesson, review the writing circle rules earlier agreed upon by the class. Ask individuals to give themselves a value for each rule, perhaps a number from 1 to 5 or a word value ("good" or "could improve"). They may record their ratings in their journals.

Based on your own classroom observations, you may or may not agree with each student's assessment. If you do not agree, you have an opportunity for a brief conversation or short note about why your opinions were different. Students may not recognize their own contributions, perhaps because of comparing themselves to others who seem to be more successful or confident. Or, some may not see ways in which their improved behavior could benefit the writing circles.

Discussing How to Respond and Share

Students may discuss how to respond to works-in-progress and then how to share works-in-progress in writing circles as one combined lesson or at two separate times. In any event, the group roles identified on the role cards at the end of Chapter 1 will work effectively in this activity.

Learning Goals: To develop skills in responding to works-in-progress in writing circles; to develop skills in sharing works-in-progress

Part 1: Determining Roles

Invite your students to form writing circles.

Give each writing circle a set of four role cards: discussion leader, note taker, time keeper, and speaker. Either appoint a leader or ask for a volunteer. The leader will see that the other roles are assigned.

Distribute or display the poster of advice "Responding in Writing Circles" (see page 21), or once writing circles have fully responded to that poster, turn the class's attention to "Sharing in Writing Circles" (page 22). Reduced versions of the posters appear below.

Responding in Writing Circles

Use these strategies when responding to works-in-progress in your writing circles.

Begin positively.

Comment on writing successes.
Help to put the writer at ease.

Listen thoughtfully.

Concentrate on the reading.
Consider what works and what doesn't.

Invite the writer to read aloud.

Ask a writer to choose an effective scene to read aloud.

Read aloud from the work-in-progress.

Ask a writer for permission to read aloud a strong scene.

Be truthful and tactful.

Give sincere praise—false praise is not helpful.
Be considerate and polite.

Make your response constructive.

Remember that the writing is not finished and that the writer is looking for ways to improve it.
Be supportive and offer a revision idea without telling the writer what to do:
"When you do your next draft, you could think about …"

Limit what you say.

Explain one thing you enjoyed.
Consider offering a question that suggests revision.

Do not tell a writer what to write.

Remember that the writer is in charge of choosing what to say.

Sharing in Writing Circles

Use these strategies when sharing your works-in-progress in writing circles.

Decide what you want to know.

Make a brief list of questions for others to consider.

Organize your writing.

Be sure that your draft writing is clear and well organized.

Practise for reading aloud.

Read over your writing before reading aloud the whole thing or an excerpt.

Choose your time.

Feel confident about your writing.
Be ready for the responses of others.

Choose your audience.

You may form a writing circle of people you trust.
You may meet with one classmate or with your teacher.

Choose how you will share your writing.

Read aloud and ask questions.
Give copies for silent reading and then lead a discussion.
Give copies for silent reading and then ask for written responses.

Part 2: Writing Circle Discussion

The discussion leader invites members of the writing circle, one at a time, to choose one piece of advice and comment or ask a question. For example, if responding to works-in-progress is the focus, one student may consider the idea that false praise is not helpful and comment: "I can always tell when people are pretending to like something when they really don't. I can see it in their eyes." Similarly, if the focus is sharing works-in-progress, a student may think about the idea of offering a question that suggests revision and then ask: "How can a question suggest revision? Would it be like saying, 'Have you thought about how to use commas?'"

The discussion leader would make sure that each question is addressed by keeping the conversation on that topic until the student who posed the question gained a clear understanding.

If, at the end of the discussion, any pieces of advice have not yet been covered, the discussion leader would focus the talk on those topics.

Part 3: Advice Slogan

Slogan on responding:
Listen with your ears and your mind.

Slogan on sharing:
izedganordis—No!
organized—Yes!

Following the discussion, distribute one "post card" to each writing circle—lined recipe cards work well. You will also want to make sure that dictionaries and thesauri are within easy reach of each group.

Using the notes made by the note taker, the writing circle decides on one piece of advice that the group believes is especially important. Circle members then make up a slogan about that advice, perhaps using alliteration, rhyme, or any other attention-grabbing technique. For example, a writing circle focused on responding to works-in-progress may agree that the most important piece of advice is "Begin positively." Their slogan: *Encourage. Enable. Enlighten.*

Part 4: Sharing Slogans

Create a display area in your classroom. When all the groups have finished making their slogan post cards, invite the speaker from each writing circle to say the slogan out loud and explain how it connects to the advice. The speaker would then add the slogan to the display.

Ensuring Constructive Responses

If you find that students tend to be either too polite or too negative to be helpful in their responses to works-in-progress, you may want to implement this lesson. It offers students an opportunity to consider what is involved in giving constructive responses to works-in-progress. This exploration is best begun in a context outside of their own writing and with the participation of the whole class.

Lesson Goals: To help students realize the value of making constructive responses to works-in-progress; to provide students with experiences in making constructive criticisms

Part 1: Compliments and Criticisms

Begin by asking the students to write on separate pieces of paper one compliment and one criticism about a published text they have recently read. They may already have these noted in their journals and can just recopy them. Require that they offer a specific example in order to be clear, for instance:

- "The ending was the best! If you missed one very important clue, you wouldn't be able to figure out what happened. I won't tell you the clue or it would spoil the book for you. Ha."
- "There is too much description of what the fog looks like. (I stopped counting when I got to 12.) There's no action to get you into the story."

Collect all the compliments in one bag and all the criticisms in another. Redistribute them by having students draw one paper from each of the two bags.

Begin by hearing the compliments. Invite at least 10 students to read aloud the compliment papers they drew from the bag and to suggest whether the language is clear, honest, and polite. If the language does not meet these expectations, challenge the class to think of a better way to say the compliment. Hear a few suggestions aloud.

Follow the same procedure with at least 10 criticisms.

During this whole-class discussion, list on the chalkboard or on a flip chart all the topics of students' written responses. Common ones include catching the reader's interest, using description, ending in a satisfying way, developing character, developing plot, making effective word choices, having humor, and featuring suspense. This student-generated list can serve as a reminder of the various elements of writing to consider when responding to draft pieces.

You may want to compile the list on a handout for students to keep in their journals.

Part 2: Connecting Published Texts and Works-in-Progress

Invite students to comment on the similarities and differences in responding to published texts and to the works-in-progress of peers.

The most obvious difference that will come out of the discussion is that a person making comments about a published text is not face to face with the author. There is no personal connection and, therefore, less need to be cautious about negativity. In either case, though, students should use appropriate classroom language.

Another key difference is that published texts are finished. Other than when subsequent editions are printed, professional authors don't get the chance to go back and make their texts stronger; in the classroom, however, students are working through the process and still have a chance to incorporate worthwhile suggestions.

Remembering that works-in-progress are not finished works is important. Suggest that students express criticisms in ways that leave plenty of room for the writer to consider writing that doesn't work for specific reasons. Such comments as "When you do your next draft, you could think about ..." or "Before you finish this scene, ask yourself" are supportive and constructive, and recognize that the ideas, sentence structures, and words are still inside the writing process.

Part 3: Standing in Another Writer's Shoes

To provide students with more experience in considering constructive responses, you could have them turn to their own draft writing. Invite them to find one area in their writing that they see as needing revision. Then, as if they are responding to someone else's work, have them write a comment that is honest, but discouraging. This activity is safe in terms of writer's ego because students are responding to something that they have already recognized as needing revision and it's in their own writing.

You will likely find that many students are keen to share these comments aloud due to the humor element in this activity. You needn't ask them to change the discouraging comments to constructive ones that are honest and polite—most students will get the point immediately.

Be sure to remind students about appropriate language use just in case their sense of humor overcomes their sense of what's expected in your classroom.

Reading in Writing Circles

Reading and writing are partners in literacy where both inform and inspire the other. The writer and the reader both focus on the same things: the alphabet, words, sentences, paragraphs—pages and pages of meaning. All writers learn from reading the works of others.

Throughout the lessons in this book, especially in Chapter 5, specific strategies are offered for you to encourage your students to make connections between their reading and their writing. In this lesson, the focus is on encouraging students to read widely and to think about their reading choices.

Learning Goals: To give students opportunities to consider a wide variety of reading choices, select their own reading materials, and reflect on their personal reading choices

Part 1: Book Browse Introduction

Offer students a wide range of reading choices, perhaps selected from the school library or from an approved resources list. It may make the reading choices more appealing to your students if you display only three to five copies of any one title rather than setting out a class set.

Explain to your students that a Book Browse is an activity that gives readers a chance to take a quick look at a variety of reading choices. There are many ways in which students can become familiar with texts and gather enough information to make thoughtful choices. Depending on what type of text they are looking at, these strategies may be useful:

- Read the title and the name of the author: students do read titles, but may not pay attention to the name of the person who wrote the book.
- Look at the details of the front cover illustration: designers take great care to choose visuals that connect meaningfully to the text.
- Read the blurb on the back of the book: the blurb is intended as a brief snapshot of the book to entice the reader.
- Read the copyright date and place of publication: some students like to read classics while others prefer more current titles; readers may want to read around the globe or choose books published closer to home.
- Read the first paragraph or first page: knowing the initial direction and tone of a book provides the reader with a clear sense of whether it's a good book choice.

- Read a page chosen at random: this sampling gives the reader a sense of the author's style and theme.
- Read information given about the author: certain details about the author may draw readers into the book: these may include home, interests, and previous books written.

Briefly explain these Book Browse strategies to your students. They may have more ideas to offer.

Part 2: Considering Choices

Ask students to prepare a page in their journals with the heading Book Browse. Explain that they will record the titles and authors of several books used in this activity. They will be given about one minute to consider each book choice. After the timing, they will write a brief note to answer the question: Is this something I would choose to read? Why or why not?

Part 3: Books, Books, Books Within Writing Circles

Ask students to form writing circles of five to seven people—larger groups work better for the sharing of resources.

Stack the reading choices, one copy of each, in front of or on the floor beside one student in each group. This person will be the group leader. You may want each stack to have the same book choices, but that is not necessary. A varied selection conveys the idea that there are lots and lots of great reading choices. For a group of five students, it would be good to have a minimum of at least 10 books in the stack of choices. The more choices, the better!

Join one of the writing circles.

Ask the group leader to randomly distribute one reading choice to each person in the group.

Give a one-minute time limit for everyone to quietly look through this first reading choice. (Reassure students that there will be time to talk with others later.) You may decide to give a bit more browsing time than one minute if you notice that most people are quietly engaged in the task. Then, as voices begin to whisper, call out, "Time's up." At this point, there is often informal chat. Without discouraging this too much, move things along by asking students to record brief comments in their journals.

Each person passes the reading choice to the right, and the leader takes another selection from the original stack. Proceed as with the first reading choice until you sense that everyone has looked at enough choices (perhaps 5 to 8). It's worth keeping this activity going as long as most students show an interest. Usually, the informal conversations between timings will generate interest in the choices; eventually, students will be passing materials across the group or asking to see a choice someone else has looked at.

Part 4: Making Choices

Explain that you require everyone to have at least one reading choice decided upon within a certain time limit, perhaps a day or two. Most students will make their choices immediately, but others may want to check out other sources—home, school library, or local library—or take time to think about the selections you have offered.

Ask students to record their final decisions in their journals with the following details included: title, author, copyright date, place of publication, and clear explanation as to why this is the best reading choice.

Part 5: Time to Read

In our classrooms, we must show that we value reading by setting aside class time for quiet reading. You might want your class to decide on a certain block of time that they can count on for reading each day or so many minutes per week.

Explain that you expect everyone to read outside class time, as well. It is important to clearly define your expectations—perhaps 30 minutes every day. When students get hooked on reading, they will often forget about minimum requirements and read voraciously.

You may wish to encourage daily reading by asking your students to write brief notations in their journals every day, indicating how much time was spent reading and also commenting on how they are enjoying and understanding their reading choices. You could write brief replies, especially for the first few times.

January 14

Last night I read for almost an hour. If I didn't have so much math to do, I would've read a lot more. This book is really good so far because of how you know something's happened and it's something about a black horse, but you don't know what. I wonder if I have to wait until the very end to find out.

An hour! Great! I guess math deserves your time, too. You'll soon find out part of the mystery, but this author keeps you guessing almost to the very end. Have fun wondering!

When students say that they are not keen about particular choices for whatever reason, offer the option to choose something else. Perhaps you can help with this new selection. If, for example, a student reports that the text is too complex, you may know of something similar in theme, but less difficult.

At the beginning and end of each reading time in your classroom—whether it's 10 minutes, 30 minutes, or more—allow for informal chat. Take time to eavesdrop on conversations as well as to ask a few questions about how the reading is going. Mention how you are enjoying your own reading choice and how much you're reading each day. Doing so will help give the class a sense that all of you are in the same reading community and it may perhaps lessen any sense of reading-as-homework.

The books selected in the Book Browse become a very important writing resource for your students in developing their writing. They provide examples of effective word choices, correct usage, and various writers' styles.

Books that captivate a reader may also inspire that reader to be a writer!

4

Facing the Blank Page

How do writers find themes? How do writers begin to develop those themes? In our classrooms, blank pages will remain blank unless each writer is inspired to engage in the writing process, with all its excitement and its disappointments.

One of the most significant ways to inspire and engage your students is to help them to find their own themes, rather than to suggest themes that you hope will be meaningful to them. This chapter offers several lessons that are designed to help students face blank pages with enthusiasm and with confidence within their writing circles.

Exploring Theme Choices

Many of the ways students can ease their way into writing are the same for fiction as for autobiographies. Lesson structures in this chapter apply to both fiction and autobiographies. The structures can also be readily adapted to such text forms as newspaper articles, essays, letters, and poetry.

Writing has a purpose. We write to communicate, sometimes with others (sharing ideas and expanding our understandings) and sometimes with ourselves (exploring understandings of ourselves and the world around us). When we write, we want to write about things of interest to us—ideas that we care about and that have specific meaning in our lives. We may choose to do so through imaginary experiences.

When we write about our own lives, we gain a clearer understanding of ourselves and those closest to us. As students approach transitions in their lives, writing autobiography can be especially significant. For example, moving from one grade level to another can be a significant transition for younger students; junior high students are very reflective as they prepare for the larger world of high school.

The best way to tap into our students' own themes is to invite them to brainstorm for ideas. The writing circle is an important part of this first challenge of facing the blank page.

Learning Goals: To consider a variety of personal themes or experiences and to choose one; to think further about the chosen theme or experience in order to see a clear writing purpose

....

Part 1: Making Choices

Invite everyone to form writing circles.

Ask students to write the numbers 1 to 3 down the left-hand margin of a page in their journals. Beside each number, they write one thing they have been recently thinking about or talking about—an idea that they'd like to continue to think about or talk about. Give a minute or two for this personal brainstorming. As students record their themes, you will be free to write your own.

Then, ask everyone to scribble out the numbers and renumber the three ideas in the order of importance for today. This step provides an opportunity for writers to think more critically and to make decisions about exactly which theme matters most to them.

Ask students to draw a line under the brainstorming: I often use that line drawn across the page as a reminder to the writers that the activity is changing in some way. Then, have them write and respond to this prompt: *A theme I'm interested in writing about is …* Here, the students are moving from considering choices to making a clear statement about a theme choice—a decision is made.

> Most students will choose topics that will interest them for a while. However, if students take the simple, small step of thinking of what to write about "today," it may not seem to be an onerous task.

Part 2: Affirming Choices

Invite students in their writing circles to take turns saying aloud the themes they have chosen. The sorts of themes students choose include the destruction of wildlife habitat, how family members support one another, and the responsibilities of pet ownership. Be sure that everyone respects the option not to share, though. Tell students they may share their chosen theme by saying it aloud in their writing circle or simply say, "Pass." You could encourage them by first sharing the theme you have chosen to write about.

No explanations of the themes are given. Throughout this quick oral activity, there should be no comment by you or by students in the writing circles. This is the first opportunity to voice aloud a writing topic—quite an empowering thing for those who *choose* to do it. It helps writers to understand that what they choose to write about is their own responsibility, not something dependent on the approval of anyone else. However, even if no one chooses to identify the writing topic this first time, that is okay. Maybe next time, more students will be ready to share.

Part 3: Freefall About Setting

> Freefall is stacking lumber, mortar, and bricks from which to build.
> —W. O. Mitchell

> For writing autobiographies, simply ask students to choose actual places that are or have been important in their lives. It may be helpful to direct their thinking to places they have enjoyed, safe places of fond memories. Some students, however, may have chosen themes that are more difficult to write about and you will need to support them.

It isn't always true that writers know why they are writing about a particular topic; however, it is true that writers will write more clearly and with more energy when that purpose becomes obvious to them. Help your students to "wade into" their chosen themes by doing some activities that explore the ideas further. Freefall writing is a simple start.

Explain that for five timed minutes, students will freely write in their journals about a place or setting connected to their chosen themes. Before you begin the timing, provide a few moments for writers to get organized and, perhaps, to establish in their minds what place they will write about. Find your own comfortable writing space, as well.

Then, give the instruction to begin. Throughout the five minutes, avoid any temptation to look around to check whether or not students are writing. If they are not writing, they will at least see you and others busy doing so. It is my experience that, eventually, everyone writes.

When the five minutes are up, tell students they may finish an idea or a sentence before they stop writing. Then, ask them to quietly reread what they have just written. If some whispering begins, ask for quiet so as not to disturb others. At this point, all students need to spend time thinking about their own writing.

The First Timed Writing

If this is your students' first timed writing, ask them to count the number of words written. Tell them to count even the words "a" and "the," as well as any words crossed out.

When the counting is completed, begin by asking people who wrote 10 or more words to raise their hands (this usually means that everyone raises a hand). While all hands are still up, add more to the count: 20, 25, 30, 40, 50, 60, 65, and so on. Students will be interested to see who still has their hands up as the number of words increases.

Finally, ask those who wrote a lot to explain how they were able to do so. Others will listen carefully and learn from their classmates. In the next timed writing, you will most likely see earnest concentration in all writers.

Part 4: Consider Setting

Ask your students to look back to find one strong word, phrase, or sentence in the freefall writing about setting. Have them underline that strong writing.

Then, ask them to look back to find one weak word, phrase, or sentence. Have them circle that weak writing.

Both activities ensure that the students are not only thinking about the theme and the setting, but also considering word choice and writing style—what works and what doesn't.

Part 5: Affirming Setting

Just as it was worthwhile for your students to have a chance to say aloud the themes they had chosen, so it is worthwhile for them to share aloud other aspects of their writing. It reminds writers of their ownership of the writing and helps to make that personal connection clearer and stronger as the writing develops.

Invite your students in their writing circles to say aloud the setting, again giving them the option to pass. Add to this the option of sharing the strong writing. For example, a student may say: "The setting I wrote about was a place where a stream goes through the woods. And I like when I wrote 'small bubbles swirled past.'" It is not important, here, for students to explain why they considered the writing to be strong. It's enough to hear these samples of strong writing aloud.

Part 6: Oops! That's Gotta Go

It is also important to invite students to say aloud the writing they considered to be weak. The first time I did this with my class, I had not expected them to find the activity so funny. The writers shared without embarrassment, always laughing along with the rest of their groups. We all write terrible stuff in draft writing. Why not laugh about it? Laughter is an indication that we have some understanding as to why the writing is weak.

You may want to begin by sharing with the whole class a genuine example from your own writing—you won't need to make one up. When I wrote *We're Friends, Aren't We*, the editor responded by saying that my first pages were "slow." I knew that was her polite word for "boring." Because I really liked my main character and knew him well, I found the first scene where he decided to give up smoking very interesting. The editor, however, helped me see that a reader wouldn't have that same enthusiasm for my character right away. I needed a new beginning for my novel—one that wasn't "slow."

Note that this isn't a threatening experience for the writers because they are deciding what writing is weak and can choose whether to share or pass. Some students gain confidence from hearing their teacher and those they think of as skilled writers admitting to having written something that doesn't work well.

Part 7: Why This Theme?

Students will sometimes write about what worries them and about what makes them sad. Support those students by having private conversations about when they might want to share in their writing circles and when they might prefer to share with a trusted friend. In rare cases, students will want to share only with you, their teacher. These students will still benefit from the discussions and other activities in their writing circles.

To conclude this exploration of theme choices, ask students to think about why their chosen themes are important to them and to answer this question: Why am I writing about this theme?

Give a two-minute timed writing for them to freefall about this question. Although some people may know right from the start why they are interested in specific topics, others may discover their reasons only by thinking further and by writing.

At the end of the timed writing, ask everyone to underline one word or one phrase that zeroes in on the main reason why. Some may decide to chat in their writing circle about their reasons, while others will want to keep their thoughts to themselves.

Exploring Character and Theme

"Exploring Character and Theme" builds on "Exploring Theme Choices." It applies equally well to the writing of fiction and to the writing of autobiography.

By the end of the lesson structure "Exploring Theme Choices," most students will want to write about the theme or experience they have chosen, but may not know how to develop their writing. It takes a while before a writer is committed enough to dedicate the time and energy it takes to push forward past those blank pages and the disappointments that inevitably accompany the elation of writing successes. This lesson will bring writers closer to that commitment.

Learning Goals: To further develop writing topic; to engage students more fully in their writing; to recognize that dialogue helps to reveal character and add interest to writing

Part 1: Looking Back

Invite students to form their writing circles. As always, this may mean shifting furniture around to form the circles or prompting students to move from one table to another to join the circle of their own choice.

Ask everyone to take a few quiet moments to read over their earlier writing on theme choices, setting, what works and what doesn't, and why the theme is important to them. This quiet beginning gets students back into a writing mood and provides an opportunity to further reflect on the writing. Some will get a clearer sense of where their writing is going.

Part 2: Thinking About Character, Thinking About Self

Ask students to think about the setting they wrote about in the last lesson and to imagine a character in that setting. Prompt them to consider these two questions: Who is this person? What is this character thinking about? If the focus was a real place that has been important in their lives, prompt students to consider these two questions instead: How old were you at that time? What were you thinking about?

Have students write for five minutes, answering the appropriate questions. As they begin to write, they may drift away from the specifics of those two starter questions, yet they are still moving forward in their writing. After this timed writing, you may decide it would be helpful to repeat the activity of counting words—some students will still need a reminder to concentrate during freefall.

Invite students to talk about what they have written in their writing circles; they may also pass, if they prefer. Discourage them from simply reading their freefall notes aloud. Freefall writing is intended as author's notes. It has not been revised for an audience, so ideas may be disjointed and incomplete. When writers consider what they have written and then describe their ideas aloud, they will more fully understand their writing.

Part 3: Drafting Conversation, Remembering Voices

Ask students to imagine their new character having a conversation with another character in the same setting: "Who is the character talking to? What would these two people talk about?"

Before students begin, tell them to follow these two important rules:

1. Only write the words the characters speak—no descriptions of scene or action, no naming speakers with "he said" or "she said," no sounds except the talking.
2. Forget all the rules about writing dialogue except one: when a new person speaks, begin a new line.

Explain that following these two rules will speed up their thinking so that they can focus on hearing the voices in their imaginations.

You may prefer to do a quick review of the rules for writing dialogue before telling students to forget all the rules but one. Ask them to open books they are currently reading to a page where characters are having a conversation. In

If the focus is autobiography, prompt students to remember a conversation with another person in the setting or about an event that happened in that setting: "Who is that other person? What did you talk about?"

their writing circles, have them come up with rules about writing dialogue. Some will notice that there are quotation marks that identify words spoken aloud; others will see that the speaker is named occasionally, but not always; the fine points of punctuation will also be discussed. For the sake of speed, ask them to do this orally in just 60 seconds. Hear one rule from each circle until all key ones have been reviewed; then, continue with the lesson.

Part 4: Reading Aloud—Whole-Class Writing Circle

When characters speak, we learn so much about them and what is going on in their lives. This whole-class activity gives your students a chance to share their writing with others and to learn about how character is revealed through dialogue. Although small-group writing circles will later do this activity, it is helpful to do one or two examples with the whole-class writing circle because the activity is more complex than some.

Invite one or two writers to read their conversations aloud to the whole class. Remind them to read only the words spoken. No introduction of setting or character is permitted before the reading—the conversation must "speak for itself." You may want to read your conversation as the first example.

After each reading, ask others to tell the writer something that was revealed about the character. For example, someone may offer: "Your character sounds like a determined type of person because she talked about how she wasn't going to give up volleyball just because of bullies."

You may find that a few quiet seconds are needed before the next person responds. Encourage responses by asking questions: "What mood is this character in?" "What is the relationship between the two speakers?"

Finally, give the writer a chance to say whether the ideas are close to what was expected for the character. If they are not, the writer, without any prompting, will understand that the dialogue needs to be clarified or extended.

Part 5: Reading Aloud—Small-Group Writing Circles

Invite students to continue this same activity in their small-group writing circles. You may want to appoint a discussion leader or to ask for a volunteer in each group. Discussion leaders ask questions intended to encourage others to respond. As you move from circle to circle, you could offer your own responses as well.

This is usually a very lively activity, perhaps because students are becoming more relaxed about sharing and more committed to their characters or experiences. Of course, students still have the option to pass.

Part 6: Quiet Time Options

Conclude this lesson by offering quiet time for writing or reading. Students may want to continue writing their conversations (perhaps now adding descriptions, actions, and so on) or they may want to read over their writing. A third option, as always, is for them to enjoy a few pages of a book they are reading. You could suggest they read text with lots of conversation and consider how the author revealed character through dialogue.

Thinking Through Images and Words

The early writing stages must include time to think—time to daydream. Wayson Choy, the Canadian author of several acclaimed novels, describes his subconscious as "where most of my writing takes place." Our conscious efforts to develop writing are very important, too.

Your students, with their often fast-paced lives, will benefit from structured thinking activities, such as the one suggested in this lesson.

Learning Goals: To reflect on a specific character or personal life experience; to more fully understand the character or the experience, the theme, and the writing purpose; to create a collage that represents a fictional character or personal life experience

Part 1: Selecting Images and Words

Whenever you use magazines, be prepared for a temporary mess. It would help to keep things organized if you require that students take turns getting magazines for their group, returning magazines when the group is finished, and putting discarded scraps of paper in the garbage or recycling box.

Ensure that you have on hand a supply of old magazines. Your students may have some at home to donate, or you could ask your local library for magazines they no longer want in circulation.

Invite your students to form writing circles.

Ask one person from each writing circle to get magazines and possibly scissors for their group. You may choose to ask students to tear out images and words, and then later use the scissors to trim.

Ask everyone to find at least a dozen images or words to use to make a collage that represents the fictional character created in the last lessons *or* the personal life experience chosen for an autobiography. This will take at least 20 minutes, with lots of chatting and exchanging of magazines. It is during this time that students are reflecting on their characters or experiences, making decisions about what best represents them. The subconscious is likely busy as well, just as Wayson Choy described.

Part 2: Collage and Caption—First Draft

Students will loosely arrange the images and words on the table in front of them to form a draft of the collage. (The trimming with scissors and pasting happens later.)

Next, they will think of an appropriate caption for the collage and write a first draft.

Part 3: Explaining the Collage and Caption

In the writing circles, each person explains how the images and words connect to the character or experience, and then reads the draft caption. This talk will help the writer more fully understand the character or experience and may also help in the decision to keep or discard any images or words. Reading aloud the draft caption will help the writer decide if revisions are needed.

Distribute colorful sheets of paper. From these students may choose backgrounds for their collages. Be sure that each writing circle has enough scissors and glue to share.

Students create final drafts of their collages and captions. If they choose, they may display them in a certain area of the classroom. Require that all collages be saved for use later, whether they are on display or not. When students complete their writing, their collages can be used as cover pages or as illustrations within.

More Activities to Foster Writing

If your students would benefit from further activities designed to help them develop various aspects of writing fiction or autobiographies, you may want to draw on the following brief summaries of lessons for your writing circles.

Fiction

Setting as Character: Offer students this scenario: Imagine your character in a particular place and in a specific mood. Write a description of that place. Now, change your character's mood. Write a description of *the same place*, reflecting the changed mood. Have students share in their writing circles and discuss how the description of the setting changes.

Window Shopping: Offer students this scenario: Imagine your character walking down a street or in a mall. A display in a window catches her/his eye and the character stops to look closely. Describe what is in the window display. Think about why that would make your character stop and look. Have students share in their writing circles and discuss how character is revealed by what characters do.

Letters or E-mails: Offer students this scenario: Imagine that your character receives a significant letter or e-mail message. Write the one received and then write the reply. You may choose to do more than one exchange. Have students share in writing circles and discuss how character is revealed by what characters write.

Alternative Scenarios: Writing circles may want to create their own scenarios to write about. Perhaps after you have asked them to do one or more of the activities suggested above, you could invite each group to write another scenario on a recipe card. These cards can be displayed for all writing circles to use.

Getting Started: Ask writing circles to find three stories or novels all of which have different types of beginnings. Encourage them to use books they are reading. During this task, the students will talk about whether certain beginnings are the same or different, reading aloud to one another. It doesn't matter which beginning styles they find—it's the talk that will help them to develop an understanding of the options they have when they begin their own stories. Students then make brief notes in their journals to describe three beginnings and comment.

Your students may already feel committed to their writing. When you see that this is the case, it's time to get out of the way and just let them write.

> *Sample Writer's Journal Entry*
>
> **How authors begin:**
>
> 1. **A lot of books start with describing a scene. I only like that if it's not pages and pages of description.**
> 2. **We found a book that started with a character talking. That was interesting because the character was asking about a missing person.**
> 3. **The start I liked best was the author telling what a character is doing. It's like you're watching them and they don't know it.**

Autobiographies

Interview: Ask students to talk with someone else—for example, a family member or a friend—who has shared the same experience they want to write about. Doing this may give writers a different slant or provide them with more information to consider for their autobiographies. Suggest that writing circles brainstorm for people students might want to interview and questions they might want to ask. Students would then make notes in their journals.

> *Sample Writer's Journal Entry*
>
> **I could interview my older brother and my grandmother. Some questions I could ask:**
>
> **Do you remember teaching me to skate? (Jeff)**
>
> **Was I a good skater? (Jeff and Nan)**
>
> **How did you make my skating skirt and jacket? (Nan)**
>
> **Do you remember anything funny that happened at the rink?**
>
> **Hint: I crashed into a certain person. (Jeff)**
>
> **Do you remember taking me to the Fantasy on Ice when I was six?**
>
> **What kinds of things did I say? What did I eat? (Nan)**

Approve the questions before interviews begin. Doing this ensures that everyone will ask worthwhile questions and remember to follow them up by asking for details.

You may want to review interview techniques, discussing how interviewers don't simply ask a list of questions; by listening carefully, they may change and expand the ideas of the interview. Here is a chance for some role-playing to practise interviewing skills.

Storyboard or Timeline: Suggest that students create a storyboard or a timeline to visually make clear the beginning, middle, and end of their autobiographies. Writing circle members may share their series of draft illustrations or timelines. This discussion will help writers to further clarify their ideas.

Focus Photograph: Suggest that writers find a photograph that connects with the experience they are writing about. The photo, perhaps a scan rather than a treasured original, may help them to focus on something, for example, the mood they want to create. In the writing circles, students share their photos, explaining the connections to their writing. This discussion will help writers to further develop their ideas. The photo can later be used in the finished autobiography. Again, the option to pass is available.

Published Authors as Writing Partners: Ask each person in a writing circle to choose the *first page* of one autobiography to read and analyze. Your school librarian could help in this activity by making a text display from which students may choose. The greater the variety of choices in the writing circle, the better. Students will make brief notes in their journals to answer these questions:

> Did the author begin by writing about the present time or with a memory from the past?
> Did the author begin by telling something about himself/herself or by telling about someone or something else?
> How did the author catch the interest of the reader on the first page?
> How many sentences on the first page started with "I"?
> What one word on the first page seems to have special meaning to the author?

When everyone has the notes ready, the writing circles can begin their discussions. Each person will present findings, making sure that others have time to comment or ask questions. You may want a discussion leader, note taker, and a timer to keep each group organized throughout this discussion.

Meeting Writing Goals

By now, students may have chosen themes, written about settings, drafted conversations, and made collages and captions—all ways to get into their writing and past a blank page. Perhaps they have also worked with some of the writing development options identified above. They are now ready to write page one (or paragraph one) of their stories or autobiographies and more.

Students do not have to write complete stories or autobiographies in order to learn the skills involved. For fiction, they can develop a scene that they imagine to be part of a short story or a novel, exploring character and plot

Some writers may choose not to do a storyboard or timeline; they may be able to shape their autobiographies by continuing to write a first draft and then looking at organization later. Still, these writers will benefit from writing circle discussions of other people's storyboards or timelines.

development, description, dialogue, and so on; for autobiographies, as well, they can focus on a particular incident, considering different perspectives and perhaps interviewing others who took part. Writing one scene rather than a longer text will make the task much more manageable. It may also inspire students to keep on going once they experience success.

Students will have a variety of choices to consider as they begin writing. Require that they set up a personal goals calendar, perhaps using either the template for fiction (see page 45) or the template for autobiographies (see page 46). Their calendars should reflect writing in class and outside class time, perhaps at home or in your school library during lunch break or after school. Either template may be helpful as writers consider what they have accomplished so far and set goals for continuing. When tasks are completed, students can check them off the list. On the lines provided, they write the dates they have set.

You will notice on the templates that students are to submit their writing for comment before they submit it for assessment. This sequence lets you read the writing as any other reader would, rather than as an evaluator. I find that students are more open to suggestions about correcting and revising after I have read and responded to their writing on a more personal level.

The comments you give at this earlier stage may be similar to these:

This reminds me of a book I read about a girl who ran in a race even though she wore a brace on one leg. Your character showed the same kind of determination.

I was hooked right on your first page, wondering why your character couldn't remember who his brother was.

Your story has such a sad ending. I didn't want the dog to die. Yet, it is a very realistic ending because sometimes vets just can't help animals after an accident.

To spread out your marking load and to give you time to enjoy reading each story or autobiographical scene submitted, you may want staggered deadlines. Simply divide your class alphabetically into as many groups as you wish: perhaps A–G, H–M, N–S, and T–Z. Then, stagger deadlines, being sure to rotate the group that is expected to be earliest.

Encourage your students to have reasonable expectations for themselves, giving lots of time for ideas to grow. Post "an expiry date" to indicate your own goal for having all these scenes submitted for assessment. Most students will choose this deadline, but some set their deadlines earlier.

Each time your students begin a new writing project, they will have to face those blank pages. Brief activities that explore ideas and writing directions will help to make those blank pages less daunting. I'm not really sure that it gets easier each time, but experienced writers do have the advantage of knowing that, eventually, one page gets filled, then the next, and the next …

My Writing Goals: Fiction

For my story, I already have …

- ☐ chosen my theme
- ☐ written about setting
- ☐ written a conversation
- ☐ made a character collage and caption
- ☐ written about window shopping
- ☐ written e-mails from characters
- ☐ decided how I will begin

Next, I will …

write the first page by _____

finish the first scene by _____

finish the first draft by _____

edit and proofread by _____

share with my writing circle by _____

finish the second draft by _____

submit for comment by _____

submit for assessment by _____

My Writing Goals: Autobiography

For my autobiography, I already have …

- ☐ chosen my theme
- ☐ written about setting
- ☐ written a conversation
- ☐ made a collage and caption
- ☐ made notes on an interview
- ☐ made a storyboard or timeline
- ☐ decided how I will begin

Next, I will…

write the first page by _____

finish the first scene by _____

finish the first draft by _____

edit and proofread by _____

share with my writing circle by _____

finish the second draft by _____

submit for comment by _____

submit for assessment by _____

5

The Author as Writing Coach

Earlier in this book, I described reading and writing as partners in literacy, each informing and inspiring the other. This idea was first made clear to me during a summer writing session at The Banff Centre. Award-winning author Alice Munro, one of our workshop leaders, gave this advice: "When you're not writing, read."

Yet, the curriculum outcomes for reading and writing are usually defined separately in education documents; professional development initiatives generally focus on reading *or* on writing. This separation may imply that these are not intrinsically connected. In our classrooms, we often describe one class period as a "writing time" and then another as a "reading time." (When I was a Grade 8 student, the separation was even greater: my English teacher had separate class periods for spelling, grammar, writing, and reading. There was little writing time—we were more often occupied with fill-in-the-blank grammar exercises.)

My own experiences as an author and as a reader have taught me that I learn to write by writing and by reading, and I learn to read by writing and by reading. When I write, I use the alphabet to form words and I use those words to form sentences, paragraphs, and chapters. When I read a published work, I'm reading the finished product of an expert author who has gone through the same writing process. As I read, I consider and compare—I absorb style, form, word choices, and so on. What I learn transfers to my own writing, just as my writing brings me closer to understanding how and why an author makes certain choices in theme, imagery, sentence structures, and more.

In our classrooms, we cannot assume that students, on their own, will make these reading–writing connections. This chapter offers strategies that will give your students opportunities to make clear, perhaps even insightful connections between their own reading and their own writing. As they gather in their writing circles, it should be as natural for students to grab the texts they are reading as it is for them to grab their draft writing, a pen or pencil, and their journals.

You may want to select from these lessons, or you may find it useful to adapt the ideas to your specific classroom needs. For example, one lesson describes writing circle activities designed to encourage students to explore correct punctuation usage in writing dialogue and to generate rules together. This same framework can be applied to any aspects of grammar, punctuation, sentence structure, and usage.

Strong Beginnings

Richard Peck, a Young Adult author from New York City, made a one-day visit to my Grade 7 classes when I was in the earliest stages of my own writing career. One specific detail of his presentation made a deep impression on my students and on me: he told us that he would rewrite the first page of every novel at least ten times. He explained the importance of first impressions and of hooking readers on page one.

This lesson focuses on strong beginnings in fiction writing, but the strategies can be adapted for use with other types of writing, including non-fiction, essays, and newspaper articles. You will need to present the activities over a few days or even longer.

Learning Goals: To develop further understanding about effective story beginnings; to write effective text beginnings

Part 1: Read Silently and Make Notes

Invite your students to form writing circles and to bring books they are reading with them.

Distribute two sticky notes to each student. The student rereads silently the first page of a novel, thinking about how the author has created an effective beginning—in other words, ways in which the author has hooked the reader. The sticky notes are used to label any two examples of effective writing on that first page: a student first places the sticky note next to the effective writing and then jots a brief explanation on the note. These are examples of notes students could make from their observations:

- mystery in the first sentence
- lots of good description
- someone shouts and you wonder why

Part 2: Sharing Ways of Hooking the Reader

One at a time, students in their writing circles take turns sharing what they have noted about effective writing, reading aloud the ideas on the sticky notes and reading aloud brief excerpts from the novels. When finished sharing, each person will place the sticky note near the centre of the group's table. If another student has identified a similar idea, the sticky note is placed on top. Repetition, in this instance, is a good thing because it will reinforce the idea that many authors use similar techniques on their first pages. The layering of the sticky notes creates an easy visual to illustrate this point.

When all the sticky notes have been placed, ask students to decide upon a label for each group of sticky notes. Using the examples above, students might use these labels: mystery, description, and shouting. It doesn't matter which words they choose to describe how the authors began their novels as long as there is an obvious connection to the writing. The point of the labelling is for students to recognize patterns in how authors begin their stories.

After this initial sharing activity, ask one person from each writing circle to put the sticky notes (still grouped) on a common display, perhaps a flip chart or the chalkboard, and write the labels underneath. Students from other writing circles will place notes with similar ideas on top of those already on display. The wording of the labels may not be identical, but they will form an interesting collage or list describing the same idea.

Invite one student to come to the common display and count how many times each way of hooking the reader was used. Put the totals above the grouped sticky notes. Students may be interested in a whole-class discussion about which technique is used more often and why, or which techniques are favorites.

Finally, to close this part of the lesson, ask students to reflect in their journals about which first-page technique they enjoy most when reading and which they have used or would like to use in their own writing, briefly explaining why.

Part 3: Modelling on Strong Beginnings

You may want to do Part 3 of this lesson in another class. It is always a good plan to give lots of time for thinking and then come back to ideas when they are fully digested. Meanwhile, keep the sticky notes and labels on display.

Draw attention to the sticky-note display of first-page techniques. Perhaps encourage students to share any reflections from their journals.

Invite students to form writing circles, either the same as for Part 2 of this lesson or with two people from each writing circle moving on to another one.

In their journals, students write the title and name of the author. They then copy, word for word, the first sentence or two of the books they are reading. Require that they use quotation marks around the sentences quoted. Recording, rather than simply reading the first sentence or two, adds more to the learning experience. Students slow down and are more thoughtful as they write. Word choices, punctuation, the rhythm of the sentence, and more—all these become clearer in the writing.

Students must now carefully consider that first sentence or two and notice as much as possible. They needn't write answers to these questions, but you will want to support them by giving an indication of what they are looking for. Here are some suggestions:

- sentence length: Is the first sentence short, average length, or long?
- content: What is this sentence about?
- word choices: Are there simple words? complex ones? Is there a lot of description? Are there action verbs or quieter, being verbs?
- punctuation: How does punctuation lead the reader smoothly through the sentence?
- tone: What mood or tone is set by this beginning sentence?

Now, students are ready to model on strong beginnings.

First Sentence Modelling

A student using my sports novel *Out of Bounds* might record these notes in his or her Writer's Journal:

Title: *Out of Bounds*

Author: Sylvia Gunnery

First sentence: "The time on the scoreboard blinked red, high in the corner of the gymnasium: 1:03."

My own sentence: The time froze on the clock at the end of the rink when the referee blew the whistle: 1:01.

Consider inviting students to write a complete paragraph following from their own sentences. They may or may not want to use these paragraphs—the choice is their own; however, their journal notes and sentences or paragraphs will serve as helpful resources.

Each student takes turns sharing in the writing circle by showing the chosen novel to the group, reading aloud the author's first sentence or two, and then reading aloud the new sentence.

Part 4: Commenting on How First Sentences Hook Readers

Students read the first pages of their own draft writing and think about the techniques they used to begin their stories or scenes. Considering ideas learned earlier in this lesson, they will now decide whether their writing should be revised in order to hook the interest of their readers. Some confident writers will find that their first-page techniques already do a good job of hooking readers, while those who recognize the need for change will now take time to revise.

When everyone is satisfied that their story or scene beginnings are effective, it is time to share with the writing circle. On separate pieces of paper, students record their own first sentences or even first paragraphs. The papers are passed to the right until every member of the writing circle has read and commented.

Remind students of the necessity to comment thoughtfully, politely, and honestly (see the boxed comments below). Because these sentences have been revised after much discussion about strong beginnings, it is quite likely that most comments will be positive and encouraging. You will find that such comments from friends are often saved as treasures. When writing slows down or even stops, rereading these notes can encourage students to push through writer's block.

Sample Story Beginning with Writing Circle Comments

Kenny walked behind the vice-principal, thinking about how short the man was and how shiny his shoes were.

- **This is so good. I mean it. Right away you know Kenny is in trouble.**
- **I like the part about how the vice-principal is short because it's like Kenny is taller and he's looking down on the guy.**
- **I'd say this would be better for the second sentence maybe. The first one could be more about who Kenny is. But I like it the way it is now too.**
- **I get the feeling that Kenny was in trouble before because he's just thinking about the vice-principal and not about what might happen to him. I want to read your whole story.**

Before ending this lesson, ask students to record in their journals any two things they have learned from this experience of modelling on the work of published authors. The limited notation requirement means that they will be able to jot down ideas quickly. These notes can be a reminder of even more concepts learned during the discussion.

Righting Writing

The best time for an individual student to learn a specific rule about correctness in writing is during the writing process. Personal connections and immediacy are two important ingredients for learning. Although there will be times when mini-lessons with the whole class are appropriate, your students will also develop skills in spelling, grammar, sentence structure, punctuation, and usage by selecting a problem area from their own writing and seeing how published authors avoid the problem.

One of my students, for example, complained that he was overusing "and." Good, I thought, he has already recognized the problem. Now, to fix it. I asked him to look at any page in the book he was reading and to count the number of times that author had used "and." He then counted the number of times he had used it on a page of his own draft writing. He quickly did the math: "Oh man, I got 11 more."

My challenge to him was to revise until he had close to the same number as the published author, using similar sentence structures. In effect, the author becomes a writing coach. With a little help, the student's overuse problem was solved.

Learning Goals: To learn matters of correctness from published authors; to develop revision skills; to create a Righting Writing poster to share

Part 1: Published Author as Writing Mentor

Invite your students to form writing circles.

Ask them to look through their own draft writing to find and highlight one problem in grammar, punctuation, sentence structure, or usage. In the case of students who don't know where improvements are needed, you or another member of the writing circle may offer help. Then, have students search in published texts to find how the authors avoided the problem.

Perhaps a student uses a comma incorrectly to connect two sentences. (The door slowly opened, the shadow came into the room.) In a published text, this comma splice error would not likely occur, so the student should be able to find instances where two related sentences were correctly joined. Options include these:

- The door slowly opened and the shadow came into the room.
- The door slowly opened; the shadow came into the room.

Modelling on the published texts, students revise to correct their writing problems. In their journals, notes are made to explain the problem and how it was corrected. Examples from the draft writing can also be included for further clarification.

When everyone in a writing circle has had time to search, correct, and make notes, each person takes a turn describing the problem and explaining how it was corrected. Others will jot brief notes when the problems described are ones they find in their own draft writing.

Part 2: Righting Writing Poster

Skills learned in Part 1 can be shared with the entire class. Ask students to make colorful Righting Writing posters which perhaps could be added to a common binder or put on a classroom bulletin board. Each poster explains one correctness rule, shows examples, and includes a slogan that will help others remember the rule. Sample text appears below.

Righting Writing

its and it's

its = ownership
The dog lost its ball.

it's = it is or it has
It's going to rain today.
It's been raining all day.

Its or it's?
Just stop to think
about which one fits.

When other students in your class make the same errors, invite the person who created the Righting Writing poster to give a one-on-one lesson to explain how to make corrections. As these students work together, you'll be free to continue conferring with others.

Developing Vocabulary

Readers can be like sponges, soaking up new vocabulary and noticing innovative use of language. The activities in this lesson encourage your students to be word sponges.

Learning Goals: To develop a vocabulary with a greater variety of words; to develop a vocabulary of more complex words; to develop an understanding of root words, prefixes, and suffixes

Part 1: Word Analysis

Invite your students to form writing circles. Be sure that a dictionary and a thesaurus are close at hand for every writing circle.

Briefly review these concepts: root word, prefix, and suffix. One way to reinforce this is to have a 30-second race to see how many prefixes and suffixes students can list individually.

Next, prompt students to search through books they are currently reading. Each person is looking for a word of more than three syllables. In their journals, the following are noted:

- the word of at least three syllables
- the root of the word
- a prefix, if any
- a suffix, if any
- the sentence in which the word is found
- an original sentence using the word correctly

When all students in a writing circle have analyzed their words of at least three syllables, everyone takes turns sharing.

Sample Writer's Journal Entry

Word: humiliating

Root word: humiliate

Prefix: none

Suffix: -ing

Author's sentence: "It was humiliating to have the same schedule as a bunch of strangers."

My sentence: It was humiliating when I was teased about my freckles.

Part 2: Word Banks

Encourage your students to keep lists of new words and of spelling corrections in their journals. Require that they now add at least one new word to their word banks, selecting from the ones presented in their writing circles. Because they have just heard extensive explanations, simply recording the new word is probably sufficient. Some may jot reminders about meaning, if they wish.

Next, ask students to visit others in the class, selecting more words to extend their word bank lists to ten. Encourage them to choose words they think they will use, to ask for correct pronunciation, and to talk about meaning. This activity is somewhat chaotic, but it's constructive classroom chaos because the conversations will be about new words.

Part 3: Word Play

Puzzles: Challenge writing circles to create a word puzzle, such as a crossword or word search, using the words they have added to their word banks. This process takes about an hour, perhaps more, so plan to continue the activity into another day. Ask that each group make an answer guide for the puzzle created. After you have checked for correctness and for clarity, the writing circles will be ready to make master copies of their puzzles.

When all the word puzzles are ready, make multiple copies of each, but not necessarily one for every student in your class. You may want to set aside a block of time for everyone to do puzzles, or you may decide to keep these puzzles on display so that students can occasionally take a break from other activities and do a puzzle.

Spelling Bees: Spelling bees provide further opportunity for word play, especially if the game is not threatening to those who find spelling difficult. Play the game with three levels of word difficulty:

- definitely easy (one point)
- average (two points)
- challenging (three points)

Give each writing circle 15 pieces of paper cut into small rectangles. Ask them to look in their word banks and in the books they are currently reading to find five words for each of the three levels. This activity generates a lot of conversation about what makes words easy or harder to spell and can informally offer valuable lessons in spelling.

As your students are finding words for the spelling bee, label three plastic zip bags for easy sorting and storage of the words: Definitely Easy; Average; and Challenging.

This spelling bee is a whole-class activity. You may want each writing circle to be one team, or you may decide to combine groups to have fewer teams in the spelling bee. Let some students be scorekeepers, judges, and the person who gives the spelling words.

Students decide which level of word to spell. This choice factor helps to ensure that no one feels threatened or embarrassed in the game. Also, teams may use the three levels as part of their strategy to earn points. One team may, for example, choose a Definitely Easy word if they are winning and the game is

If anyone tries to help a speller or disturbs the game in any other way, you or a student judge can give that team a one-point penalty.

coming to an end. Another team may decide to ask for Challenging words when their score is falling behind and it's worth the risk to earn three points.

To be sure everyone listens carefully during the spelling bee, you may offer other teams a try when a word is misspelled. If a word worth two points is misspelled the first time, the next team can try spelling it for one point less. There can be three tries to correctly spell a three-point word.

Comparing Writing to Writing

Forming words into sentences, sentences into paragraphs, and paragraphs into pages seems so easy for the writers of the books we read. Each of their ideas develops clearly and connects smoothly to the next one. There is variety in their structures and surprises in syntax and diction. Students are often inspired to be stronger, more artful writers when they notice the techniques used by professional authors and apply some of them to their own writing.

Learning Goals: To develop skills in sentence structure; to develop skills in paragraph construction

Part 1: Comparing Paragraphs

Invite your students to form writing circles.

Review how authors connect ideas in a sentence with joining words and with punctuation. Depending on the experiences of your students, you may choose to begin with common joining words, such as "and," "so," or "because," and the simplest punctuation, such as periods or commas; or, you may decide that your students are ready to learn about more complex joining words, such as "therefore," "on the other hand," or "hence," and punctuation, including the semi-colon and the dash.

Ask students to open their books to a page they have already read and to select any page from their own draft writing. Everyone looks for the longest paragraph in each source.

For easy comparison, students then make notes in two columns in their journals: My Draft Paragraph and The Published Paragraph.

- How many sentences are in the paragraph?
- Were any sentence beginnings the same? If so, how many?
- How many words are in the longest sentence?
- How many joining words are in the paragraph?
- How many times did the author use punctuation to join ideas within sentences?
- Name all the types of punctuation used in the sentences.

Within their writing circles, students take turns sharing their findings, describing similarities and differences in styles. This discussion will generate lots of questions and explanations about sentence and paragraph development. Students sometimes work out explanations together; however, when they are stuck, they can ask for help from the teacher. Here, they won't be learning the labels for sentence structures—they are learning to create the various sentence structures using joining words and punctuation.

Part 2: Plans for Revision

Ask writers to make notes in their journals about revising sentence structures and paragraph construction. The template on page 59 or one similar may be useful.

This analysis of sentence and paragraph construction can be used during assessment discussions between you and individual students. The writer can point out earlier draft writing where problems existed and then show current draft writing where improvements have been made. Parents will appreciate seeing this record of skill development as part of the communication between school and home.

Part 3: Making Revisions

Having noted and discussed plans for revision, the logical next step is for students to implement these revision ideas. With the support of their journal notes, the writing circle, and the teacher, students will now find this job fairly easy.

Speaking of Dialogue ...

As was demonstrated in "Righting Writing," where individuals compared their own writing to that of published authors and constructed grammar rules, students may devise grammar rules and teach them to others. In this lesson, writing circles work together to discover the grammar and punctuation rules that apply to writing dialogue.

Learning Goals: To develop correctness skills in writing dialogue; to construct rules for correct use of punctuation and capitalization in writing dialogue

Part 1: Questions on Dialogue

Invite students to form eight writing circles. Ask all of them to reread a page of fiction that has a significant amount of dialogue.

Distribute one dialogue question card to each group (see next page for a selection of eight questions). You may also want to use the role cards introduced in Chapter 1 so that each person in the writing circle has a specific responsibility. Students work together, studying the published pages of dialogue to come to a clear and correct answer to the question on the group's card. This activity usually takes about ten minutes.

Dialogue Question Cards

When is a comma used in dialogue?	When is a period used in dialogue?
What is the purpose of indenting in dialogue?	When is capitalization used in dialogue?
When is the speaker identified in dialogue?	When is the speaker <u>not</u> identified in dialogue?
Where are quotation marks placed in dialogue?	Why is dialogue used in a story?

Part 2: Preparing to Teach

Having clearly and correctly answered the question about dialogue, each writing circle now has the responsibility of designing a lesson to teach others what they have learned. Every lesson plan should include

- a rule for writing dialogue, based on the question
- an example of how this rule is used
- a visual to illustrate this rule
- an assessment to be given to the teacher and to at least one person in each of the other groups

The visual can be any object with qualities that remind people of the ideas in the rule. For example, a group planning a lesson on the use of commas in dialogue may show (or draw) a pause button on a remote control to represent the function of the comma.

Sample of a Student-Generated Assessment

1. **Did you understand our lesson?**   1 2 3 4 5
2. **Did you learn anything new?**   1 2 3
3. **Were our voices clear and interesting?** 1 2 3 4
4. **Did you understand our visual?**   1 2 3
5. **Was our visual a good idea?**   1 2 3 4 5

                   TOTAL = ___ out of 20

Please write comments or suggestions on the back.

Require that the lesson plans be approved by you. It may be best to do the presentations on another day, giving time for all groups to fully prepare.

Part 3: Teach and Learn

Each writing circle teaches a lesson, with students sharing responsibilities in ways they work out together. During the presentations, students in other groups will make notes in their journals about what they learn. As each lesson is finished, those who have been given the assessments will make their responses.

Part 4: Dialogue in Draft Writing

As a follow-up to this activity, encourage students to reread their own draft writing and decide whether there is enough dialogue and whether the rules for using dialogue have been followed.

The journal notes that students have made will be helpful as they work on dialogue in their draft writing.

The five lessons presented in this chapter suggest only a few ways in which your students can learn by carefully considering published texts. In the next two chapters, further reading–writing connections are outlined to encourage revision and to explore voice.

Comparing Writing to Writing

Text I compared my writing to: _____

After comparing my writing to the author's published writing, I realize that I need to revise by

☐ improving variety in sentence length

    I have too many   short   average   long   sentences.

    I don't have enough   short   average   long   sentences.

☐ improving variety in sentence beginnings

    I begin with this word too much _____

    I begin with the subject too much _____

    I begin with an introductory phrase too much _____

    _____

☐ using joining words more effectively

    joining words I use too much: _____

    _____

    joining words I could use more often: _____

    _____

☐ using punctuation more effectively in longer sentences

    punctuation I use too much: _____

    punctuation I could use more often: _____

6

Where Does Revision Fit?

The complex question in this chapter title can be answered simply: revision fits everywhere. The writing process is a bit like driving around the block again and again—each time you see the same scenery, but slightly differently. This circular process builds layer upon layer of writing development and of writer's understanding:

- *Immediate Revision:* Writers make changes as they go. They look back on words, for example, written two seconds ago, and ask: Are these words correctly spelled? Have they been used correctly? Are they effective?
- *First Reread:* When a page or a paragraph or a scene is finished, writers reread to make sure they've said what they wanted to say in the way they wanted to say it. By now, purpose can be clarified: Why am I writing this? Who is my audience?
- *Further Rereads:* There is no magic number for how many times a writer will reread works-in-progress; however, it is certain that all published authors comb through their works page by page many, many times.
- *Revision After Conferring:* Writers' noses are pressed to the mirror of their work—they're so close that they can't see clearly. Writers need other, more objective pairs of eyes to help them see ways to improve.
- *Revision to Get It Right:* Eventually, every word must be correctly spelled; every sentence and paragraph must be constructed clearly and effectively; every dot, line, and curve of punctuation must be placed appropriately.
- *Final Revision:* When a writer has a sense that the work is ready for an audience, it's time for that slowed-down-to-a-crawl revision. In the publishing world, manuscripts are sent back to authors to check before the pages go to print. This is the last chance for finishing touches, corrections, and changes, so writers must be thorough.

Keys to Encouraging Revision

When first drafts are completed, students often have a strong sense of satisfaction, of having worked hard and accomplished what they had set out to do. The last thing many want to think about is revisiting the writing to make changes and even cut whole sections that aren't effective. Yet, ultimately, that's just what writers have to do.

In my experience, these are the keys to encouraging revision:

- *Ownership:* Students will revise more and learn more about revision when working on their own writing projects—be sure not to overlook this truth. Using exemplars as a revision exercise can be worthwhile when activities are very brief and when the students move directly to their own writing to make comparisons. However, unless the writing is their own, students have little reason to care about whether it is the best it can be.
- *Writer's Purpose:* Unless writers have clear understanding about why they are writing specific pieces, they are less likely to care about making improvements. This idea of purpose is not about completing a school assignment—it's about why a writer has chosen this particular topic to write about in this particular way. (More details about writer's purpose are given in Part 4 of "It's All Fixed" below.)
- *Timing:* Until first drafts are complete, it's best to avoid the temptation to point out areas that need to be revised or corrected unless students have asked for input. Ideas need to fill those blank pages—achieving that is difficult enough for many young writers without their being blocked by concerns about revision. Encouragement is important in the early draft stages—save the corrections and improvements for later.
- *Time for Distance:* Without enough time for rethinking, revision, and rewriting, writers won't get the necessary distance from their own work. This distance provides objectivity, a chance to step back and recognize what is being written and whether or not it is communicated clearly and effectively. Writers benefit from setting projects aside for weeks or even months, then coming back with new energy to rethink, revise, and rewrite.

The lessons suggested in this chapter will encourage students to revisit works-in-progress and to use various revision strategies to make improvements draft by draft.

"It's All Fixed"

In our classrooms, students are more likely to see revision as "fixing mistakes" in spelling, grammar, and punctuation. To some extent, they are right, but this kind of revision is the easiest part of the process: we have computer tools, dictionaries, thesauri, and other writing resources, such as guides, to help us make corrections.

Students need to think of much more complex matters as they revise, especially in early drafts. It doesn't make much sense to clean up mistakes in spelling, punctuation, syntax, capitalization, usage, and so on, if the writing itself is going nowhere. Ideas need to be revised. Inconsistencies need to be noticed and eliminated. Whole sections may need to be lifted from one part and placed more effectively in another.

This lesson will help your students to focus on some more complex revision strategies.

Learning Goals: To build skills in clarifying theme; to build skills in organization; to build skills in essay development

Part 1: Where Am I Going?

Invite students to form writing circles, bringing with them a double-spaced first draft of an essay.

Distribute two brightly colored crayons or highlighters and one sticky note to everyone. Each student chooses one color that will represent the theme or main idea of the essay. Ask everyone to

- find a single word in the first paragraph that best represents that main idea
- underline or highlight this word in color
- find the sentence in the first paragraph that best explains the main idea
- underline or highlight this sentence in the same color (The word chosen may or may not be within the sentence chosen.)

Students pass their draft writing to another member in their writing circles. This person reads the colored word and sentence and uses the sticky note to comment on whether or not the main idea is clear. If the idea is clear, the reader will restate it in different words to show clear understanding. If it is not clear to the reader, the reader will ask the writer a specific question beginning with "Do you mean …?" The question gives the writer and the reader a chance to talk and to check their understandings. I have often overheard a reader say, "Oh, I get it now," and the writer then knows that a change is not needed.

Two examples of comments are given below.

| Your essay is mainly about how pets are part of the family, just like people are. | Do you mean that people who play sports make higher marks than if they don't play sports? |

When the essays are returned with the notes, some students may need time to make revisions for clarification, perhaps by having a conversation with the person who wrote a question on the note. Writers may know what they are trying to say and believe that their ideas are clear. In conversations with readers of their first-draft writing, however, they may learn that others do not understand. The readers can point out the words or passages in question and explain exactly where the confusion lies.

Part 2: Staying on Topic

Now the writers are ready to reread their entire essays. Their task is to consider whether every idea and the supporting details offered are clearly connected to the main idea or theme of the essay.

Each student will need a second colored crayon for this activity: the color used to show the main idea will now be used to highlight or underline all the ideas that develop this theme; the other color will be used to indicate all the supporting details—explanations, anecdotes, and examples that expand on the ideas. Ideally, the entire essay will be highlighted or underlined in a clear balance of ideas and of supporting details.

For example, a paragraph within an essay begins with this topic sentence: "Cats and dogs need to be inside when there's a storm, just like children." The student highlights it in blue. The student then works with a second color, green, and highlights sentences about a pet not knowing how to find places to stay warm when it's snowy or howling uselessly on the front steps when in danger of frost bite. As the student looks at the paragraph closely, she finds that one sentence does not seem to fit—it is unrelated to the main idea: "Deer sometimes eat our tulips when it's spring." This still-black sentence would likely be deleted.

The first time I did this coloring activity with students, I watched crayons flashing back and forth across pages, one color and then the other. At a glance, I could see whether individuals in writing circles had stayed on topic with a balance of ideas and supporting details. One student, though, had no color added after the second paragraph. "I got off topic. Three whole pages wasted!" After a brief conversation, he decided to scrap the original topic and write a new opening paragraph to introduce the main idea that he had developed throughout most of the draft. Problem solved.

Part 3: Sharing Our Learning

When all the coloring is completed, students will be ready to cut ideas that don't fit, to add more ideas and details when necessary, or perhaps to construct a new introductory paragraph. Before this work begins, ask students to explain in their journals what they learned about essay writing by using colors to deconstruct their draft essays and to outline one specific revision they plan to improve their essays.

In the writing circles, each student takes a turn showing the colorful draft essay and explaining one thing learned by using the colors. It's important that students do this without simply reading aloud their journal notes.

Create a display area on a flip chart or chalkboard. Ask each writing circle to choose two examples of lessons learned from the coloring activity. The students who first presented the ideas will write them on the display. This display may serve as a writing resource for students to consult as they do necessary revisions.

Part 4: Double-checking Purpose

As already stated, writers will more easily move into the next stages of developing their drafts by thinking about purpose: *Why am I writing this?* Some people know the answer to this question from the very beginning, but it is worthwhile rethinking and restating purpose just to be sure and clear.

Ask writers to make notes in their journals to answer that crucial question: Why am I writing this? Remind students that they are digging deeply into their own personal purposes here, not simply writing because they're at school and assignments have to be done. In other words, the question truly is, Why am I writing *this*?

Students may share with others in their writing circles. For those who decide to share, they will find it very satisfying to explain their writing purposes to others. Doing so also helps them think critically about purpose and more fully understand their writing.

This Stays … This Goes

Students learn by reflecting on writing that is successful as well as writing that needs to be improved. We're teachers—we want to help students understand what is wrong and how to improve; however, it sets a positive tone when we begin with compliments about writing that works well. We can then move on to make suggestions for improvement.

Learning Goals: To develop an understanding that revision is a positive process; to learn to recognize writing successes; to learn to recognize writing that doesn't work

Part 1: Revision Math and Mess

Invite your students to form writing circles, bringing with them draft work that has been revised and proofread. The mess of revision must be obvious on the draft work.

Encourage everyone to find the page in their draft work with the most changes—a constructive mess!—and to count how many changes were made. Each writing circle adds up changes made by group members and then either you or a student records the results in numerical order on a flip chart or chalkboard.

Ask each student to find the most successful change on that same page and put a check mark in the margin beside it; then, ask each student to find a change that could still use revision and to put a question mark beside it.

Challenge students to revise even more on those same pages. Although they will be working largely on their own pages, they may help one another and give encouragement within their circles. After a few minutes, ask one person from each writing circle to come to the display and change their group's original number to include the additional revisions. The nature of the revisions will vary from simple to complex, but the display promotes the idea of the more revisions, the better.

Now, on a flip chart, brainstorm with the class the *types* of changes they made during revision of their draft work. Very likely, spelling and punctuation will be at the top of the list even in higher grades. Most students have lots of experience with these.

Once the obvious types of changes have been listed, give time for students to reconsider their draft writing and revisions. Perhaps circulate from group to group, noticing significant examples of revision and offering labels, such as clearer organization, more effective word choices, and sentence fluency, to describe them.

Part 2: Revision and Proofreading Advice

Ask each writing circle to consider the discussion and revision activities just completed and to write one piece of good advice about revision: when to revise, how to recognize what needs to be revised, how to make changes that work well, and so on.

Good Advice to Consider

If you use exclamation marks too many times, you lose the effect.

Read your revisions out loud to find out if the changes work.

After every five or six sentences, think about whether it's time to begin a new paragraph.

Give enough details so the reader can picture what you can see in your mind.

Make sure all the ideas in your essay connect to your introductory paragraph.

Double-check these pieces of advice for clarity and correctness, bearing in mind that whatever the students come up with is the advice they are ready to consider.

The final draft of each piece of advice is written on plain paper with a visual to represent or illustrate the advice. The visual can be clip art, an original drawing, or a picture found in a magazine. The group that offers the advice about the use of exclamation marks, for example, could draw a large megaphone with lots of exclamation marks spilling out. Next to the megaphone could be a cartoon sketch of a person plugging his ears.

Part 3: Recording Useful Advice

Display the final drafts of advice in your classroom and prompt the students to record in their journals two useful pieces of advice from the display.

Make Light of Revision

A writer who has a commitment to the writing—who has made personal theme choices, has a clear purpose, and wants to see the project have a life of its own—can't help but revise. Revising isn't a chore. Every change feels like success.

Yet many students do not easily get to that commitment point in their writing. By offering a bit of fun with revision, we can help them experience that feeling of success.

Learning Goals: To rethink and revise draft writing; to learn new strategies for revision; to reflect on personal revision strategies; to have fun

Part 1: Create Revision Task Post Cards

Invite students to form writing circles.

Distribute a "post card" or recipe card to each group. Ask writing circles to create a revision post card listing five specific revision tasks.

Students look through their own draft writing to find places where they made significant revisions. Each person shows one example to the writing circle and the group comes to a decision about the best way to describe that specific change. When everyone is satisfied that the wording is clear and correct, the revision task is written on the post card. This process continues until the group has written five different revision tasks; all groups need to generate the same number of tasks.

> *Sample Student-Generated*
> *Revision Post Card*
>
> 1. **Correct a spelling mistake in a word with two syllables.**
> 2. **Start a new paragraph where you forgot.**
> 3. **Take out a comma that's in the wrong place.**
> 4. **Rearrange sentences in a paragraph to improve organization.**
> 5. **Fix a confusing sentence so it makes sense.**

Part 2: Revision Challenge

One person from each group delivers the revision post card to another writing circle and challenges everyone to do each of the tasks.

The writing circle works together on each task. Doing this encourages students to help one another understand what is required, how to find a place to revise in the draft writing, and how to do the revision. All writing resources are allowed in this challenge. Writing circles may call upon you to help them understand certain revision tasks, as well.

Each writer signs the blank side of the post card when all five tasks have been completed. The card is returned to the group that made the challenge as soon as all writing circle names are signed. Your students may be interested in a timed challenge, but speed isn't necessary.

Part 3: Thinking About Revision Tasks

Ask each student to note in their journals at least two of the following, giving an example of each:

- one revision task I do a lot
- one new revision task I learned today
- one revision task I find easy
- one revision task I find hard to do
- one revision task that made a big difference

Plan to look at all of them and write brief comments to encourage and maybe clarify. Teachers need to know each student's sense of personal revision successes and needs.

Sample Writer's Journal Entry

One revision task I find easy is fixing confusing sentences.
Example of confusing sentence: When Larry and Hank bumped into the two girls, they turned around and ran as fast as their basketball legs would go.
Revision: When they bumped into the two girls, Larry and Hank turned around and ran as fast as their basketball legs would go.

One revision task I learned today was to change sentences for variety.
Example of first way: It was almost midnight when they snuck back home, cutting through backyards and staying away from lights.
Revision: They snuck back home, cutting through back-yards and staying away from light. It was almost midnight.

The Whys and Whats of Writing Resources

Students aren't alone when they are revising draft writing—behind them are teams of experts ready to lend a helping hand: dictionaries, thesauri, writing handbooks, computer tools, and more. It is true, though, that many students in our classrooms don't take the time and effort to use these resources. Maybe, they just need a reminder of their inherent value.

Learning Goals: To become more familiar with the purposes of the various writing resources: dictionaries, thesauri, writing handbooks, and computer revision tools; to become more familiar with the layout and content of these resources; to recognize some differences and similarities between the resources

Part 1: Investigate Resources

Have available in your classroom multiple copies of as many writing resources as possible. These include dictionaries, thesauri, writing handbooks, and word processors (with programs that have revision tools, such as cut and paste, track changes, spell check, grammar check, and a thesaurus).

Invite your students to form writing circles.

Assign to each group the task of investigating one specific resource (more than one group may explore the same resource, if necessary). Each writing circle becomes an "expert" on one resource and will prepare a presentation for the class. Students should consider these questions:

- What are the main reasons this resource is useful to writers?
- How does the layout of the resource help writers to access information?
- What warnings might writers need to think about when using this resource?

Part 2: Plan a Presentation

A writing circle studying the thesaurus could choose a parrot, with its reputation for saying the same words over and over, as the mascot, reminding writers to avoid repeating words and to use a thesaurus to find alternatives.

Writing circles prepare presentations to teach the class about their assigned writing resources. Their presentations should include these elements:

- clear explanations about specific uses of the resource, how the layout helps writers, and cautions that writers need to consider when using this resource
- an animal "mascot" as an effective metaphor to represent the resource, with an explanation about the connections between the resource and the animal given in the presentation
- a puzzle or other type of challenge that would encourage students to use this writing resource (For example, a group studying a writing handbook may create a "treasure hunt" to find specific information using the table of contents.)
- an assessment card to be given to the teacher and to at least one person in each of the other groups

During the presentations, students will make notes about their learning, possibly under the headings Type of Writing Resource, Something I Learned, and Something I Already Knew. Anyone who has been given an assessment card will complete it after each presentation is finished.

> *Sample of Student-Generated Assessment Card*
>
> 1. Did you understand our lesson?   1 2 3 4 5
> 2. Did you learn anything new?   1 2 3 4
> 3. Were our voices clear and interesting? 1 2 3
> 4. Did you understand our mascot?   1 2
> 5. Was our mascot a good idea?   1 2 3 4 5
> 6. Was our word search interesting?   1 2 3
> 7. Did our word search help you learn?   1 2 3
>   TOTAL =   ____ out of 25
>
> **Please write comments or suggestions on the back.**

In addition to the formal lesson, you may occasionally require that students make journal entries about how they have recently used one or more of the writing resources. In their notes, they would name the resource and explain precisely what information was used, giving an example from their own writing.

> *Sample Writer's Journal Entry*
>
> **Yesterday I looked in the *Canadian School Thesaurus* to get more variety of words for my essay about how people bite their nails. I kept saying "bite" or "chew" over and over. I found other words I could use instead, like "gnaw, munch, and mangle." My favourite one was "gnaw" because it really gives a nervous feeling.**

Essay Evolution

Inexperienced essay writers may believe that their first thoughts in draft writing are in the best order, but this is likely far from true. The very act of writing clarifies understanding. As a writer begins a first draft, it can be a tentative exploration or a freefall to discover ideas. Gradually, the writer gets more solidly grounded in the topic and feels more confident about the direction of the essay. Sometimes, the best opening paragraph can be found on the last page of a first draft.

Learning Goal: To further develop skills in essay organization

Part 1: Essay Puzzle

With writer permission, you could use an essay written by a student one grade level above your class. It would be up to the student writer whether to share anonymously or not.

For this activity, it's best to use a student-written essay that has gone through all writing stages to a completed final draft. The essay should be about six or seven paragraphs long. Retype the essay with each paragraph on a separate page. The essay title and possibly the name of the author are typed on a separate page, as well.

Make one complete set of these pages for each of the writing circles in your classroom. Shuffle the pages so that the paragraphs are not in the original order.

Invite your students to form writing circles. Distribute the sets of essay pages.

Ask the writing circles to silently read the pages. Perhaps each person could take a page, read it, and then pass it to the right until every page has been read by all group members. Consider using the role cards described in Chapter 1.

Each writing circle is to determine the best order in which to arrange the paragraphs, with clear reasons why this organization is most effective. When the decision has been made, the group leader will stack the pages in order. It need not match the original order of the essay—the writer may not have chosen what others consider to be the most effective order.

> *Clothesline in the Classroom*
>
> As a way of reminding students that writing is not often linear and that organization can involve rearranging entire sections, scenes, or chapters, consider using what I call "the Carol Shields clothesline." At one of her readings, the author described shaping her novels by writing scenes when they occurred to her and then deciding later where these scenes would be placed within the whole structure of the novel. She said she imagined a clothesline where she could hang her scenes and then rearrange them in the best order.
>
> In your classroom, you might string up a real clothesline and hang a dozen sheets of paper, each a different color to represent a whole section, scene, or chapter—I like to use a bright blue clothesline with yellow and red pegs. Put this revision metaphor into motion by removing one sheet and placing it in a new position on the clothesline. Take another sheet and reposition it. The Carol Shields clothesline strategy for structuring will become perfectly clear to your students.

Part 2: Sharing Decisions

When all the writing circles have made their decisions about organization, ask for a group to volunteer to share their choice for paragraph one, clearly explaining why this would be the most effective beginning. Then, ask how many other groups chose that same paragraph to be first. Keep a tally on a flip chart or chalkboard. Prompt groups that chose a different paragraph to share their choices and justifications. Finally, make a class decision as to which paragraph will be the opening. Post it on the display and ask each writing circle to place that paragraph page beneath the title page in their essay set.

Continue discussing until all the paragraphs have been placed in order.

Share with the class the order that the author of the essay used. If the order is different, discuss whether the essay is made stronger by one or the other organization.

Part 3: Re-thinking Organization

Ask students in their writing circles to pull out their essay drafts and take as many small sticky notes as they have essay paragraphs plus one note for the title. Have them write numbers on the notes.

Students carefully reread, considering whether their paragraphs are in the best order. The numbered notes are placed on the paragraphs in the order that will be most effective for the next draft of the essay.

In the writing circles, students pass their essays to the left. Each person reads a draft essay, following the paragraph order suggested by the numbered notes. To show agreement with the suggested order, check marks are placed on the notes; to show disagreement, question marks are placed on the notes. Comments are unnecessary.

When their essays are returned, students consider the input and make their final decisions about the most effective paragraph.

Part 4: Rhyming to Learn

The reproducible sheet on page 72, "Writing Assessment," can be filled out either by the teacher or by students doing self-assessments; I like to have students do the self-assessments before I give my own responses because a comparison of our perceptions can be a good starting point for discussion.

Note that "Writing Assessment" gives lots of points for revision—students need to be encouraged to make a mess in their draft writing. A final draft may earn the student fewer points than the earlier drafts. This marking pattern supports writers who are willing to make thoughtful changes and corrections.

Ask everyone to make a note in their journals about "the most significant thing" learned about essay organization during this activity. Share these ideas in the writing circles by each person taking a turn reading the note aloud.

Invite each writing circle to choose only one of the ideas noted and use it to create a rhyme that will help others learn about essay organization. Although all the students will have recorded important ideas, "sifting through" the notes to make a choice will further develop everyone's understandings about effective paragraph order. Double-checking each rhyme for clarity and originality is a good idea.

Prompt each writing circle to memorize and rehearse its rhyme for presentation to the class. During rehearsal, encourage students to use expressive, clear voices. Some groups may want to dramatize, using props. One rehearsal may be enough. Time needed depends on the skills of each student and how playful the group becomes about the "performance."

Rhyming to Learn Samples

On Sentence Beginnings

When every sentence starts the same
that will make your paragraph lame.
Put the end at the start or the start at the end—
it's still the same message that you send.

On Organization

Organize a sentence
Word by word
To make your ideas flow.

Organize a paragraph,
Sentence by sentence
And watch your essay grow.

Organize an essay,
Paragraph by paragraph
And show us what you know.

Students may first have trouble viewing it this way, but revision is a series of stepping stones along a path to successful, completed writing. Students can feel a strong sense of satisfaction when they look back and notice all the ways in which their writing has evolved from those first ideas, through the early drafts, to that finished piece.

Writing Assessment

Author notes and other pre-writing:

□ excellent

□ very good

□ satisfactory

□ needs improvement   =   /20

Early draft writing:

□ excellent

□ very good

□ satisfactory

□ needs improvement   =   /30

Revision and rewriting:

□ excellent

□ very good

□ satisfactory

□ needs improvement   =   /30

Final draft writing:

□ excellent

□ very good

□ satisfactory

□ needs improvement   =   /20

_____

TOTAL =   /100

7

Voice and Voices

In writing workshops, we often speak of "author voice"—singular. And yes, an author does or hopes to have an individual voice, one that readers can usually recognize when they open that writer's books to any page. We notice themes, character types, word choices, sentence structures, and a certain style that a writer comes back to again and again. This author voice has been developed, perhaps even unconsciously, through unique life experiences, through attitudes, through education, and through the whimsical connection between the reader audience and the writer during the writing process.

Yet writers are not locked into one voice only. We have voices we call upon to help us connect with specific audiences for specific purposes. These are the voices we decide to use, setting a certain tone and conveying particular meaning. One morning, for example, I wrote two thank-you letters to the same school where I had given Writers-in-the-Schools presentations earlier in the week: one letter was to the students and the other was to their librarian. The voice in my letter to the students was enthusiastic and friendly. I closed with: "Have fun in school as you work toward those homework-free summer days!" The voice in my letter to their librarian was still friendly, yet had that touch of professionalism we share: "As you already know, it is a fantastic opportunity for students to make real connections with the world of writing and publishing."

The lessons in this chapter offer your students opportunities to explore and use their author voice and voices. Activities suggested will help them become more aware of the choices they make in developing all those voices.

Voices in Print

Imagine the shelves of libraries and bookstores bursting with books all written with the same voice. A nightmare! Your students will readily see the various distinctive voices of authors by reading and reflecting on a variety of first pages. Doing this will set the stage for individuals to examine their own draft writing and develop their personal writer voices.

Learning Goals: To recognize individual author's voice by deconstructing themes, characters, word choices, sentence structures, and other aspects of style; to recognize and develop personal writer voice

Part 1: Gathering Favorite Books

A few days before you plan to explore author voice in this lesson, ask each student to choose a book by a favorite author and arrange to make one photocopy of the first page of text only. When students bring you their books for photocopying, you will have an opportunity to talk a bit about their choices.

On the day of the lesson, display all the books students have chosen and brought to school. If more than one student has chosen the same book, that's okay, but encouraging diversity is worthwhile. Place the photocopies underneath the books from which they were copied, double-checking numbers to be sure each person will have one page for this activity.

Part 2: Listening to Authors' Voices

Invite your students to form writing circles.

Ask students to each select one of the photocopied pages, but not the one they brought to the display. More than one student in the writing circle may select the same author, but the group will likely find this activity more interesting if everyone chooses a different author.

Students silently read the first pages, highlighting or making notes to discover author voice. The basic question in this exploration is: What voice am I hearing? Offer the following questions to support your students as they think about author voice:

- What is the theme on this first page?
- Who are the characters? What are they like?
- What word choices reveal the author's voice?
- What is notable about sentence structures?
- What other aspects of style reveal the author's voice?

This activity engages students in deconstructing the writing.

Part 3: Let's Listen Together

In their writing circles, students will take turns sharing what they have discovered and noted. Give some classroom time for them to rehearse the reading of their one-page texts, perhaps working in partners to help each other with expression, pronunciation, and speed of reading. Each student reads aloud the first page and then describes the author's voice, giving evidence from that page of writing.

Some students may find the exploration of author voice difficult and may not be confident about describing that voice, but others in the group will be able to add their own comments to help.

Consider keeping the books from which the students copied first pages on display for others to check out. Some may be inspired to read more, following their writing circle discussions.

How Some Students Described Author Voices

Grade 4 student: My author is funny. She says students were "fizzy as root beer." A character in this story writes books and his last name is Inkpen.

Grade 6 student: The author is writing just like the character talks. There are long sentences that have a lot of "ands" so it seems like she wants to tell you so much she can't stop to breathe. But there are some short sentences that make it seem serious. One example is "Meanwhile, my cousin was disappearing." I'd say the voice is excited and serious.

Grade 8 student: This author has a tense voice. You know something bad is going to keep happening in this book. Some sentences have long descriptions that make you feel tense. "He knew that tangle of emotions well, the sudden transformation from shock to stormy outrage that left you weak and hollow inside, like those Hallowe'en pumpkins that little kids still carved." Then he writes in chopped up sentences that should've been joined together. "He grinned. Leaned back. Wound up for the throw." That gives the tense feeling too.

Part 4: Personal Writer Voices

Now, your students are ready to consider their own writer voices. Ask each student to select a page of draft writing that clearly shows personal writer voice. Some will find pieces right away while others will have to search more thoroughly through the writing. These students may need help from you: "Here's 'you.' Listen to this … Now, doesn't that sound like you?" Once students hear that whisper of personal voice, they have a starting point to begin further development. Selecting the page of draft writing that clearly shows personal writer voice may take a bit of time, so assign the task and wait to continue this lesson on another day.

You may want to work with some students to help them strengthen their author voices by doing some revision *before* meeting with their writing circles (see the text box on the next page). Should you have some writers who lack confidence, remind them of the option to pass when it's their turn to share. Listening to the writing of others and being included in the discussions may help those students gain confidence and understanding about how to develop their own writer voices. Soon, they may be ready to share. Even if they don't plan to share, all students select pieces of writing.

> *Revising to Strengthen Voice*
>
> *He left his friends and went over to another friend's place. He didn't want to get in trouble and they were probably going to get in trouble. That's usually what happens when they go over to the arena and it's already dark. He was thinking he had to change. Maybe it wasn't too late.*
>
> **In this student-written excerpt, the writer's voice is weak, but the reader begins to have a sense of that voice in the theme choice and in those hints of the character's thoughts. This writer could be coached to revise to create a stronger personal writing voice in these four ways:**
>
> 1. **By eliminating the repetition of "friend," "over," and "trouble"**
> 2. **By trying for more sentence variety, beginning fewer sentences with "he" and not having three compound sentences with the common joining word "and"**
> 3. **By experimenting with putting the character's thoughts in italicized type and writing them just the way the character would speak**
> 4. **By adding some detail of the surroundings as the character walks alone, thinking**

When all students have made selections of draft writing and have completed revisions (at least to the point where the writer can demonstrate a personal writing voice), invite them to join their writing circles again.

Prepare your students by suggesting that, should others not easily recognize their writer voices, the activity will still teach them something valuable: writing is not a simple and quick process—it requires that each writer be personally connected to the writing and that each writer takes care to be as interesting as possible. With thoughtful effort, all students will find their voices.

One by one, each student reads the draft page aloud without any introduction or explanation. The others in the group respond by offering their descriptions of the writer's voice.

"The voice is tough and know-it-all, like she has been through a lot and nothing bothers her. That's what your character sounds like."

"This shows a writer who notices every detail and has imagination, like seeing spirits and saying they have 'smoky bodies.'"

"Your voice has quick action and some suspense. You don't describe too much, just what the character is doing and thinking."

Just as was done when the students were discussing published authors, evidence must be given to support the descriptions.

To close this lesson, require that your students make notes in their journals to reflect on this experience of exploring published authors' voices, as well as their own personal writer voices. They may choose to think about these questions:

- What is author voice?
- How can we recognize an author's voice?
- What is my own author voice?

My experience with this activity is that students become very excited to hear others recognize their personal writer voices. For most, it is affirming and energizing.

Voices, Voices, Voices

When students have an opportunity to play with voices, they usually have no problem understanding how to shape writing to fit a specific purpose and a specific audience.

Learning Goals: To further develop an understanding of writer voice and voices; to further develop an understanding of how writers make specific word choices and style choices to suit audience and purpose

Part 1: Why Write and to Whom?

A Range of Audiences

Students will come up with ideas such as these:

my best friend
a lawyer
the principal of my school
a new student in our school
my grandmother

Invite your students to form writing circles.

Ask them to decide on what to write a letter about: the topic should be something that interests everyone. They may do this by having each person write a topic suggestion on a piece of paper and then draw from those to have one group topic. Or, individuals may offer their suggestions aloud, and the group takes a quick vote to choose a single topic.

When the topic has been decided on, the writing circle comes up with three to five different individuals (real or imagined) who will receive the letters. The individuals must be very different in age, occupation, and other characteristics. Remind students that they are creating various audiences for their letters. Each member of the writing circle outlines an individual on a separate piece of paper. Students draw randomly from the selection of audiences.

Part 2: Writing Together

Writers must stop to consider appropriate choices because, of course, the voice of each letter must be consistent.

Review some of the ideas explored in "Voices in Print," pages 73–76, to remind students that writers make specific choices with audience in mind. These include choices in words, sentence structure, and other aspects of style.

Now, students write the opening paragraphs of their letters, being especially aware of specific audiences.

When writing circle members complete those first paragraphs, the letters are passed to the left and the next person in the group begins the second paragraph by writing at least three sentences. This pattern continues until each letter has a minimum of three complete paragraphs, including a closing.

Part 3: Who's the Audience?

If any writing circles would like to share letters with the whole class, perhaps because of particularly interesting or humorous voices, set aside some time for these to be read aloud. Having more opportunity to consider voices will reinforce the goals of this lesson.

These first drafts are now ready to be shared in the writing circle.

The student who had written the opening paragraph reads the completed letter aloud. Others respond by saying who the audience is and giving evidence to support their opinion. The reader underlines and makes margin notes about the evidence given or about any inconsistencies in voice.

This activity continues until all draft letters have been read aloud and analyzed. To close this lesson, ask students to save these letters in their journals. The underlining and notes may be helpful reminders later.

Character Voices

Dialogue is one of the most difficult aspects of writing fiction—the author must "hear" all those distinct character voices and convey their individuality to the reader. In "Exploring Character and Theme," in Chapter 4, students considered dialogue by writing a conversation between two characters without adding description or action and without naming the speakers. This activity is worth repeating as a reminder of how authors develop the voices of their characters. (See pages 37–39.)

In this lesson, students will look even more closely at character voice, both in published works and in their own writing.

Learning Goal: To further develop an understanding of character voice in fiction

Part 1: Distinguishing Voices

Choose two books that you think your students would enjoy and that are written in first person from the main character's point of view. Find passages of at least three pages that clearly show the character's voice in each of these books.

Invite students to form writing circles.

Distribute the handout "Listener's Notes," explaining that everyone must listen carefully to the excerpts. (See page 85.) Either you or a student volunteer who has rehearsed will read aloud. Before reading, identify the title and author of each book, but not the character—students should not know even the gender or age of the character yet. Following each reading, give time for students to jot notes about the character in the second column of the handout and notes about how students know this about the character in the third column. A volunteer reader would still have time to jot notes.

Part 2: What Color's Your Character?

Ask students to share the ideas from their "Listener's Notes" with their writing circles. Although they may have noted different details, they will have recognized a certain type of character and that character's mood.

Following this discussion, ask the writing circles to imagine a color that would match the voice of each character and to explain why. No matter which color they choose, giving the rationale for what best represents those characters' voices will encourage everyone to think critically.

Part 3: My Character's Voice

Ask students to select from their own draft writing a brief scene that clearly shows a main character's voice. They may choose an excerpt of dialogue; or, if they have written from the main character's point of view, they may choose any scene.

Distribute new copies of "Listener's Notes" and prompt students to form writing circles.

Students take turns reading aloud their scenes, first giving the title or working title of the writing. They listen carefully to everyone's writing; but, to avoid tedium, they make notes on only two rather than on all characters' voices.

The writing circle, *without the input of the student writer*, shares notes and ideas aloud and discusses each character's voice. Again, a color is chosen to represent the character.

Students then record in their journals some ideas offered about their fictional characters during this activity.

Voice in Poetry

Poetry, although often complex with its conventions and layers of meaning, is a great genre for exploring writer voice. Students seem to enjoy examining their own emotions and questioning the world around them through the succinct medium of poetry.

Learning Goals: To further develop an understanding of writer voice; to explore personal writer voice through poetry

Part 1: Silent Freefall

Many of your students will be familiar with freefall, introduced in Chapter 4. Remind them that freefall is a pre-writing activity that quickly fills a page with ideas. Usually it is written in sentence and paragraph form, but not necessarily. In freefall, students can forget about spelling, grammar, neatness, and even making sense—they just keep on writing. There will be lots of time later for reconsidering and reworking the freefall if the writer finds something that's worth developing.

Ask students to think of a special object, something they own or imagine owning. Invite them to take a brief, silent moment to picture this object.

Now, students are ready for a timed freefall focused on their object. Remind everyone that continued silence is necessary for the concentration of every writer—any kind of noise could interrupt the imagination. I recommend a five-minute timing, but you may decide to extend that, especially if everyone is busily writing.

Part 2: Finding Poetry

Ask students to look through their freefall writing for words and phrases that appeal for whatever reason: perhaps they are descriptive, interesting, simple, or complex. Prompt them to underline these words and phrases.

On a new page, students write the underlined sections in a double-spaced list. This list is the skeleton of a poem, ready to be shaped to convey clear meaning. Now, the writers must be even more thoughtful. The themes of their poems are becoming clear, so they will begin to have a sense of audience. Encourage students to

- rearrange the words and phrases in the list

- add more
- cut some
- put in punctuation or decide not to
- form stanzas or decide not to

Ask students to slow down the poetry process by going back to their draft poems at least three or four times during the next week, making any changes that occur to them. Tell them not to write "clean" drafts; instead, let the mess build up on their pages as an indication of thoughtful revision.

After all the rethinking, revising, and rewriting are finished, fresh pages will be used to write clear, first drafts of the poems.

Part 3: Sharing Draft Poetry Aloud

At least one week later, ask students to write "clean" second drafts of their poems.

Invite everyone to form writing circles.

The second-draft poems are placed in the centre of the writing circle. Each person randomly picks one poem and then practises reading it without asking for help from the poet.

Students take turns reading the poems aloud in their best reading voices. Others in the writing circle respond by

- expressing the meaning of poem
- repeating vivid words or lines
- describing the poet's voice

Throughout the reading, the poets do not comment on their own poems. Instead, they listen attentively, making notes in their journals.

Part 4: The Next Draft ... and the Next

Students now revise their second drafts. After so much writing, rethinking, listening, and reconsidering, the poets will have a more solid understanding of purpose and audience. They may make a few more drafts, being sure to keep all of them.

Part 5: Revision and Assessment

You may decide to set a deadline for submission of these poems for assessment. Allow at least another few days for further revision. Require that each draft of the poem be numbered, with the most recent draft on top and the other drafts in order down to the freefall, pre-writing stage.

Before submitting their poems for assessment, students place a blank Comment page on top of all the drafts. They then invite three people, perhaps classmates, friends, family, or other teachers, to read the final draft poems and write comments. Before you do the marking, be sure to add your own comment as a reader.

You may find "Self-Assessment: Poetry" useful. How one student completed page 1 is shown below. A reproducible version appears on pages 86 and 87. Students fill out side one, giving you an opportunity to clearly understand their experiences with writing poetry. Students may use side two as a self-assessment before you indicate your decisions. Although you may have reasons to raise a mark or lower it, you and the student will have a clear starting point for discussion of poetry, writer voice, and the writing process.

Self-Assessment: Poetry

Poet _Daphne_   Title of Poem _Empty Home_

1. Number of drafts (including pre-writing) _4_

2. One important thing I learned about poetry during the draft writing:
   Poetry has a balanced language. Sometimes I used all words with one syllable, some with the same first letters ("Damp room, dark sky"). Sometimes I repeated phrases.

3. One thing I learned about voice during the writing circle discussion of my poem:
   I wanted the voice to be a homeless person. I wanted sadness so I used mostly words with one syllable like he was too tired and sad to talk. My group said the voice worked.

4. One thing I find difficult about writing poetry:
   Images are hard to write. I wrote "A lonely bug goes slowly by." because I thought that image would represent the lonely life of the homeless person. Most people in my group said I shouldn't have said "lonely." It makes it too obvious.

5. My most effective word or phrase is _____
   "I have no life. I have no home."

6. This word or phrase is effective because _it is the last line of the poem and it hits the reader with the idea that people need homes or else they feel like they have no life._

Poet _____   Title of Poem _____

1. Rethinking, revising, and rewriting   ___ /15
2. Clarity of communication   ___ /10
3. Effective word choices   ___ /5
4. Effective line breaks and stanza divisions (if any)   ___ /5
5. Use of poetic devices, such as these:
   alliteration
   imagery
   metaphor
   rhythm
   rhyme
   simile
   other _____   ___ /10
6. Correctness   ___ /5

Total   ___ /50

Comments: _____
_____
_____
_____

2

Writing Sideways

Margaret Laurence once said in an interview that she did not see her metaphors until reviewers pointed them out to her. This puzzled me, especially since Laurence was (and is) one of Canada's most distinguished novelists.

In my writing workshops, I wanted to find a way for writers to create powerful metaphors and to recognize them. For me, part of developing oneself as a writer is to learn to see and understand the techniques that work … and those that don't. So, I experimented by trying a "writing sideways" activity. It's an odd thing to ask writers to do, but I've found that it works to create powerful metaphors every time. Just trust the imagination … and then look back to recognize the connections between your words and your character.

Part 1: Seeing Sideways in Character

Ask your students to select one character from their draft fiction—a main character or a minor one—and to reread a scene important to the development of the story.

The writers will need a fresh sheet of paper. Keeping that scene in mind, students put themselves in that scene and "inside the body" of the fictional character. Ask them to close their eyes and concentrate for a moment or two, imagining the scene and the character's feelings.

Keeping their eyes closed, students imagine that their characters glance sideways and look closely at something. Encourage your students by saying: "What does your character see when looking sideways? Look very closely and notice as much as you can about what your character is looking at. How does your character feel right now?"

Give a few moments for everyone to study these imaginary details. It is important not to be more specific because you do not want to influence what each person is picturing.

When you think they have had enough time, ask your students to open their eyes and quietly write as much as they can about what they had imagined. Keep the classroom quiet for at least five minutes.

Part 2: Finding a Metaphor for Character

Ask students to silently reread what they just wrote, looking for and underlining words or phrases that *remind* them of their fictional characters.

When the underlining is finished, ask students to write notes explaining precisely how each underlined word or phrase connects to the fictional character. This is the deconstruction of the metaphor they just created by writing sideways.

Deconstructing a Metaphor

The sample excerpt below was written by a Grade 4 student. One of her characters, a young girl, had seen a homeless person on the street the day before. Now, she wanted to ask her parents if she could invite the homeless person to their home for dinner. The student underlined words and phrases that reminded her of her homeless character.

She turned her head and tried to look out the window. It was <u>dusty</u> and had some cracks. She couldn't really see outside. But it was sunny and there were flowers in the <u>garden that she could barely see</u>. Just some blue and yellow and red that didn't really look like flowers because of how dirty the window was.

Later, in her explanation to the class, the student made connections between the dusty window and the homeless person who had dirty clothes and face and had tangled hair. When I asked her to tell us more, she said: "It's just like my character. People can't see what he's really like inside because of how dirty he looks. Maybe inside he's really nice like a garden."

Now invite students to form writing circles.

Each person takes a turn revealing to the group the metaphor just created. The four steps involved are explaining some background about the character, telling what the character saw when looking sideways, reading aloud the underlined words and phrases, and explaining how the metaphor connects with the character.

Sometimes, writers, such as the Grade 10 student who wrote the excerpt below, will find this easy to do. The student was writing about a woman who was arriving alone at an airport, coming to the funeral of her father whom she had not seen in a long time.

> She stepped out of the plane where the ramp goes into the airport. A man was standing there behind an empty <u>wheelchair</u> that had a <u>dark grey</u> leather seat and scratched-up chrome sides and footrests. The seat was sagging as if the <u>wheelchair was used every day</u>, over and over again. For just a second she wanted to sit in that wheelchair and let someone help her make it to the funeral.

During the writing, the student saw exactly what the image of the wheelchair would mean to the character and incorporated the connection in the last sentence. The "dark grey" color clearly matched the mood of the character.

Not all metaphors fall into place so smoothly, though, but connections always appear through this writing sideways activity. When writers themselves can't see the connections, ask other students to offer their ideas. Once, in an adult evening class, a writer was working on a story about a father who did not communicate well with his family. Much of the story was inner dialogue, revealing all the things he left unsaid. In the writing sideways scene, the writer placed the father character in his workshop:

> He looked at the rows of cans and bottles on the three shelves above his work bench. Inside these containers were nuts, bolts, nails of all sizes, washers, screws, and small clamps; everything sorted and stored meticulously. No one else came into the workshop to take anything from these cans and bottles. They were only his to use.

This writer did not at first see how those nuts and bolts and nails all sorted and stored connected to her father character. Others in the class were happy to deconstruct her image and let her know what they saw:

- "These things are like his thoughts. He keeps them in containers in his mind."
- "I notice that there are three shelves, maybe to represent layers and layers of what he has kept from his family."
- "These are building materials. They secure things, hold them together. But in the containers they are useless. That is a metaphor for the father's thoughts, all contained inside, all of no use to his family. If he used them, it would build the family relations."

For me, the last comment was a fantastic insight.

I like how this activity gives writers an opportunity to see inside the imagination and to have a chance to understand a bit about how the writing process works. We learn to trust our imaginations and let go of those nagging doubts, to just write and write and write—something exciting and worthwhile will fill our pages.

Part 4: Blending the Metaphor into the Scene

Ask students to revise their scenes and use their newly created metaphors. Encourage them to think about how to blend the metaphors smoothly into the scenes so that readers can enjoy discovering the connections.

During this revision process, writers might want to read aloud to one other member of the writing circle for feedback. Give students at least a few days before requiring that clear drafts of the metaphor scenes be ready for sharing.

Create new writing circles by first collecting all the metaphor scenes. Randomly select four or five scenes (depending on how many students you want in each writing circle); the people who wrote those scenes would form one group. Continue until all writing circles are formed. At this stage in the process, it is essential to have a new mix of writers in the groups because there has already been a lot of discussion on the early drafts of the metaphors. Fresh ears and new responses will be valuable to the writers now.

Each writer takes a turn reading aloud the metaphor scene, giving a brief introduction beforehand, but not an explanation of the comparison. Others in the circle listen carefully and respond by describing the metaphor and commenting on its suitability. As others respond, the writer makes journal notes.

Extension: Picturing the Metaphor

Your students may enjoy reflecting further on the metaphors they have just created by drawing or finding an image that "pictures the metaphor." These images would make a colorful display along with the metaphor scenes and could be incorporated into final drafts.

Twenty-two years ago, I wrote a short story for the yearbook of the junior high school where I taught. I was 28 then. I hadn't yet studied writing at the Banff Centre; I hadn't yet taken myself seriously as a writer. Not so long ago, a former student gave me a copy of that story, saying that it *sounded* just like me. And it does. I can hear myself through the awkward story structure, the sometimes obvious "telling," and the embarrassing spelling and grammar errors (oh, how important an editor is!).

This connection to my writing past is more reassuring than discomforting, though—I recognize that the voice I choose when writing for young adults really is who I am ... and who I was. It isn't a surface construction, but a part of something more enduring.

Our students' writing voices may be new and may sometimes be hard to *hear*, yet they can be developed into strong, clear, and unique voices, perhaps to be found on the shelves of bookstores and libraries 22 years from now.

Listener's Notes

Title, Author, and Character	The character is a person who ...	I know this because ...

Self-Assessment: Poetry

Poet _____   Title of Poem _____

1. Number of drafts (including pre-writing) _____

2. One important thing I learned about poetry during the draft writing:

_____

_____

_____

3. One thing I learned about voice during the writing circle discussion of my poem:

_____

_____

_____

4. One thing I find difficult about writing poetry:

_____

_____

_____

5. My most effective word or phrase is _____

_____

6. This word or phrase is effective because _____

_____

_____

_____

Poet _____   Title of Poem _____

1. Rethinking, revising, and rewriting   ____ /15

2. Clarity of communication   ____ /10

3. Effective word choices   ____ /5

4. Effective line breaks and stanza divisions (if any)   ____ /5

5. Use of poetic devices, such as these:

alliteration

imagery

metaphor

rhythm

rhyme

simile

other _____   ____ /10

6. Correctness   ____ /5

Total   ____ /50

Comments: _____

_____

_____

_____

2

8

Within and Without the Circle

As your students gain in confidence and build skills in writing—and as their commitment to personal writing projects deepens—you will find that they become more and more independent as writers. They will know when to work quietly on their own writing and when to join with others in a writing circle to share and discuss works-in-progress. This balance between independent writing and learning in writing circles is what keeps the process moving forward.

The Independent Writer and the Writing Circle

You may find it helpful to require that students use a personal organization chart as they take on more responsibility for planning their own class time. Students make decisions about specific tasks they will do in a writing class and briefly record their plans.

Initial their plans, perhaps offering suggestions, as you visit each person during the class. Of course, there will be lots of room for lessons designed by you. Begin those classes by giving the title of your lesson and explaining how much time you will need.

One option always available for writers is to read, perhaps for part of the time or even for the whole class. When a student has chosen to read, you could have a conversation about whether the student has "writer's block," is making a reading–writing connection for a specific purpose, or is simply in the mood to relax and read. You could suggest writing a journal note that connects the reading to the student's writing. Here are a few prompts:

- This author's writing is like mine because …
- This author's writing is not like mine because …
- Something this author does that I'd like to try is …

Look at the next page to see how a student filled in a "Daily Writing Planner."

The "Daily Writing Planner" offers insight into how an individual student works as both an independent writer and as a member of writing circles. Here, a student named Diane is writing a story about two brothers who are in danger of growing apart because the older brother has begun to get into trouble with the police. A Young Offender at 15, he believes he's "outside the law"; the 11-year-old brother is losing his hero.

As the "Daily Writing Planner" indicates, on February 8, Diane planned to write a kitchen scene where the older brother, Jeff, comes home late at night and his younger brother has been waiting for him in the kitchen while both parents are asleep. This is a pivotal scene for the brothers.

A reproducible blank version of "Daily Writing Planner" appears on page 93.

Daily Writing Planner

Name: _Diane_

Date	My plans for today ...	Approved
Feb. 7	• Write the kitchen scene when Jeff comes home. • Read it over and fix it. • Make up questions to ask in writing circle	scg
Feb. 8	• Read kitchen scene in writing circle • Give everyone a copy of questions to answer • Read what people say and maybe make changes	scg
Feb. 13	• Find facts about young offenders and trial by judge • Start the courtroom scene.	scg
Feb. 15	• Lesson: Using the Thesaurus Effectively • Writing circle for Jenn's story	scg
Feb. 17	• Reread court scene in The First Stone • Work on court scene • Writer's Journal about Don Aker's court scene	scg

When she finished writing the first draft of the scene, Diane made up two questions for her writing circle to consider the next day:

- Did it seem as if Jeff doesn't care what Micky thinks about what he's doing?
- I wanted Micky to be more afraid than mad in this scene. Did you get that from what I wrote?

After her writing circle on February 8, Diane felt so confident about her kitchen scene that she decided to move on to the scene that takes Jeff to court to face charges. She needed to know what the courtroom would look like and what it's like to be tried by a judge. Although she had seen court scenes on television, Diane found her facts by interviewing her cousin who had recently had that experience. (She thoughtfully left his name off her planner.)

As classes work towards all the various outcomes in a language arts course, there would also be specific lessons in reading strategies, in media, or in drama.

As teacher, I presented a 30-minute lesson "Using the Thesaurus Effectively" on February 15. I had noted that many students were using a thesaurus liberally, but without considering how well their newly chosen words worked. By taking simple nursery rhymes and changing the words with the use of a thesaurus, the writing circles had some fun with words and got the point that a thesaurus offers choices, but the writer has to choose thoughtfully. At the end of this lesson on thesaurus use, Diane had time to join a writing circle to consider a classmate's question about her story-in-progress.

On February 17, Diane decided to reread a courtroom scene by one of her favorite authors, Don Aker. In *The First Stone*, the main character had caused a serious car accident by throwing a stone from an overpass. Since that character was tried by a judge, Diane knew she could pick up useful writing strategies from the author to make her own courtroom scene stronger. She made notes in her journal about Aker's writing style and word choices.

Diane's "Daily Writing Planner" reflects effective use of class time and a good blend between independent writing and writing circle activity. Something else to note is that some students, even without a homework assignment, will work on their writing projects between classes devoted to writing activities.

A snapshot in time

One way you can remind students to make the best use of their class time is to interrupt a class without warning and ask students to stop what they are doing. I call this activity "Freeze."

When everyone is still and quiet, ask them to think about where they are and what they were doing at the exact moment you said, "Freeze." Students quickly write notes in their journals to explain their use of class time. Here are some examples:

- Chris stopped mid-step as he was walking across the classroom. He noted that he was on his way to get a dictionary and even offered the detail that he needed to look up the word "academic," which he did.
- Jennifer noted that she was writing freefall about diving into the lake at her family's cottage. Freefall is the pre-writing activity she prefers when creating a poem.
- Marty wrote, "You caught me doing nothing." However, when we talked about it, he convinced me that he had been working on his story for most of the class and was just taking a break.
- Karen noted that she was looking for images in a magazine to illustrate her self-portrait poem.
- Dana noted that he was reading poetry by George Elliott Clarke, who had given a reading at our school the month before. Poetry that didn't rhyme appealed to Dana and he was experimenting with that genre.

You may also want students to assess themselves with a mark from 1 to 10. Later, when you read these notes, you will have an opportunity to compliment those who had been using class time well and to offer suggestions to those who hadn't.

Sometimes, as students are settling into a class, I whisper to one person to call "Freeze" at any time. This usually adds to the fun and is helpful when I'm busy with an individual or a writing circle.

To provide everyone with immediate feedback, you may want students to exchange their "Freeze" notes and write comments to each other. They are easily able to get to the point when friends have been productive in class and when they haven't.

Let's Celebrate!

In our classrooms, there are lots of ways to celebrate writing. Invite your students to be creative! Writing circles can work together to plan open mike sessions, book launches, writers' festivals, library readings, or student-choice writing awards. As much as possible, include invitations to friends, parents, and other staff.

We can take our cues from celebrations in libraries, bookstores, and other venues in our communities.

Open mike sessions

This is an informal opportunity for writers to get together and share their completed works, or perhaps excerpts from longer pieces.

The requirements are simple: the students will need a microphone and a podium. If the session takes place in the classroom, they will rearrange furniture and make changes that signal this is not "class as usual." Lamps for softer lighting may create the right mood, especially if it's an evening event.

It is unnecessary for writers to decide ahead of time whether to share their works or not. When one or two have shared, others will become more comfortable with the idea and can be nudged to take the mike.

Juice or water and perhaps some food can be offered at open mike sessions. Typically, students wait for breaks between readings to get something to eat—the change of atmosphere helps them see that quiet is especially important. If students decide to sell refreshments, the funds could be used to buy books for student-choice award prizes.

Book launches

This event is more formal than an open mike session. It can celebrate the work of a single writer, the works of one writing circle, or the completed writing by many or all students in a class.

At a book launch, usually someone introduces the writer and the specific piece that is being launched. If many works either from one writing circle or from students in several writing circles are being celebrated, there can be a general introduction to the event and to the writers who have works to share.

After the introduction, the writer (or writers) reads to the audience. If the classroom is being used, rearranging furniture will help to create the book launch atmosphere. Because this event is more formal, you may want to add festive decorations, such as flowers, balloons, or streamers.

Refreshments are almost always part of a book launch, with time for guests to mingle and to get autographs from writers after the readings.

It may be possible for students to make copies of their writing for sale—usual charge is a dollar or under; however, most often, copies are free. Students typically use any funds raised for a common purpose, such as buying novels or books of poetry from second-hand bookstores, buying colorful paper for creating covers, or creating writing prizes.

Library readings

Your school library is a great venue for student readings, perhaps regularly or as an end-of-term event. The change of space from classroom to library sends the important message that the writing being read aloud is special.

In the planning, someone from each writing circle volunteers or is chosen to introduce each writer, giving some personal background and a bit of information about what is to be read. This person can also be responsible for allotting time, making sure that everyone is aware of how much time they have for reading. Students who decide to participate in a library reading must prepare ahead of time, rehearsing to do their best reading.

Writers' festivals

A festival takes place over a few days or a week. Students plan a special event for each day, perhaps with each writing circle taking on the responsibility of

Once teachers and students become more familiar with festivals and see the excitement and other benefits, they may be inspired to organize a broader based festival, perhaps at school district level with a professional author as keynote speaker. An event at the district level usually takes months to coordinate.

Possible Criteria for Judging Fiction

The beginning caught my interest.	1 2 3 4
The writing held my interest.	1 2 3 4
The plot was logically developed.	1 2 3 4
The author writes vivid images.	1 2 3 4
The characters were believable.	1 2 3 4
The end of the story was satisfying.	1 2 3 4

organizing one of the festival days. Open mike sessions can be part of the writers' festival, as well as library readings or book launches.

Writing circles contribute best to the organization of classroom and school festivals. With teacher input and clear student vision, even younger students can play central roles in organizing writers' festivals.

Festivals provide an opportunity to involve lots of people, both in the school and in the community. Advertise on local radio and television stations and in the newspaper, as well as throughout your school with posters, PA announcements, and Web page updates. Friends and relatives often donate baked goods. As a teacher, you are there to offer guidance and can contribute special touches, such as small, potted flowering plants.

Student-choice writing awards

Writers may want to submit their finished works to be judged by their fellow students. This process takes several days and will require lots of classroom time for reading, deciding, and voting by ballot. The finished works may be in the same genre, but not necessarily.

Invite students to create criteria for judging (much in the same way as they decided on their writing circle rules). It may be helpful to print the criteria on the ballots as a reminder that the writing is to be judged on its own merit.

Alternatively, you may let students vote for their favorites without applying criteria. This approach emphasizes finished works as causes for celebration. Students are free to like what they like for their own reasons.

A group of students, sworn to secrecy, count the ballots to determine who the winners are in whatever categories they have decided upon.

Hold a special event to announce the winners. Perhaps more than one class will be involved … maybe even the whole school. Invite parents and other friends. Invite the local media to take photos.

Coming Full Circle

Celebrations take writers "full circle" in the writing process. Although not all writers will have works ready at the same time to share in public ways—and not all writers will want to share in public ways—celebrating together emphasizes the value of reading, writing, and working together … and it's lots of fun.

Any of the suggested events can incorporate all the curriculum goals of your language arts course. In planning and in holding celebrations, students in their writing circles are writing and rewriting, reading, speaking, listening, problem-solving, thinking critically, using technology, researching, taking notes, using writing resources, creating media texts … the literacy experiences are endless. Because they are engaged, they learn with enthusiasm and carry that learning forward to their next writing projects.

Think of the hype of a basketball tournament: posters and PA announcements advertise the events; music blares as fans fill the bleachers; supporters cheer and clap as players are introduced; there's keen concentration during the games; banners and trophies are awarded. Students, staff, parents, and friends come together after school or on weekends and share in the fun.

That's my model for celebrating writing.

Students look to us for signals about what's valuable and what's not. It is a powerful learning experience when they recognize that their accomplishments in writing are worth celebrating, too.

Daily Writing Planner

Name: _____

Date	My plans for today …	Approved

Bibliography

The books I suggest here are only some of the publications that have been especially helpful to me both as a teacher of writing and as a writer.

The first list is of professional books in which teachers share their classroom experiences and understandings. Reading these books I feel as though I am meeting new colleagues who are working, as I am, to find the best ways to teach.

The second list recommends memoirs and essays by writers about their writing and their lives as writers. Because my particular writing interests are short fiction and the novel, the books I have been drawn to are written by short story writers and novelists, especially Canadians. As I discovered from them ways in which to strengthen my own writing, I often saw ways in which to structure lessons that help my students build upon their writing skills.

Books by Teachers Who Share Their Classroom Experiences

Allen, Janet, and Kyle Gonzalez. 1998. *There's Room for Me Here: Literacy Workshop in the Middle School.* Portland, ME: Stenhouse Publishers.

Atwell, Nancie. 1987. *In the Middle: Writing, Reading and Learning with Adolescents.* Upper Montclair: Boynton/Cook Publishers, Inc.

Beers, Kylene. 2003. *When Kids Can't Read: What Teachers Can Do.* Portsmouth, NH: Heinemann.

Bennett, Barrie, and Carol Rolheiser. 2001. *Beyond Monet: The Artful Science of Instructional Integration.* Toronto: Bookation Inc.

Bullock, Richard, ed. 1998. *Why Workshop? Changing Course in 7–12 English.* York, ME: Stenhouse Publishers.

Copeland, Matt. 2005. *Socratic Circles: Fostering Critical and Creative Thinking in Middle and High School.* Portland, ME: Stenhouse Publishers.

Daniels, Harvey. 2002. *Literature Circles: Voice and Choice in Book Clubs and Reading Groups.* Portland, ME: Stenhouse Publishers.

Graves, Donald. 1991. *Build a Literate Classroom.* Portsmouth, NH: Heinemann.

_____. 1994. *A Fresh Look at Writing.* Portsmouth, NH: Heinemann.

Gunnery, Sylvia. 1998. *Just Write! Ten Practical Workshops for Successful Student Writing.* Markham, ON: Pembroke Publishers.

Lane, Barry. 1992. *After the End: Teaching and Learning Creative Revision.* Portsmouth, NH: Heinemann.

Ray, Katie Wood, with Lester Laminack. 2001. *The Writing Workshop: Working Through the Hard Parts (And They're All Hard Parts).* Urbana, IL: National Council of Teachers of English.

Books by Writers About Their Writing and Their Lives as Writers

Amis, Martin. 2000. *Experience: A Memoir.* Toronto: Knopf Canada.

Atwood, Margaret. 2002. *Negotiating with the Dead: A Writer on Writing.* New York: Cambridge University Press.

Findley, Timothy. 1990. *Inside Memory: Pages from a Writer's Workbook.* Toronto: HarperCollins.

Laurence, Margaret. 1989. *Dance on Earth: A Memoir.* Toronto: McClelland & Stewart.

Welty, Eudora. 1984. *One Writer's Beginnings.* Cambridge, MA: Harvard University Press.

Woolf, Virginia. 1978. *A Writer's Diary.* London: Triad Grafton Books.